CALIFORNIA

BY
ROBERT HOLMES

Produced by
Thomas Cook Publishing

Written and updated by Robert Holmes
Photography by Robert Holmes, Fred Gebhart and Maxine Cass
Original design by Laburnum Technologies Pvt Ltd

Editing and page layout by Cambridge Publishing
Management Ltd, Unit 2, Burr Elm Court,
Caldecote CB3 7NU
Series Editor: Karen Beaulah

Published by Thomas Cook Publishing
A division of Thomas Cook Tour Operations Ltd
Company Registration No. 1450464 England

PO Box 227, The Thomas Cook Business Park, Unit 18,
Coningsby Road, Peterborough PE3 8SB, United Kingdom
E-mail: books@thomascook.com
www.thomascookpublishing.com
Tel: +44 (0)1733 416477

ISBN-13: 978-1-84157-687-9
ISBN-10: 1-84157-687-5

Text © 2006 Thomas Cook Publishing
Maps © 2006 Thomas Cook Publishing
First edition © 2004 Thomas Cook Publishing
Second edition © 2006 Thomas Cook Publishing

Project Editor: Diane Ashmore
Production/DTP Editor: Steven Collins

Printed and bound in Spain by: Grafo Industrias Graficas, Basauri.

Cover design by: Liz Lyons Design, Oxford.
Front cover credits: Left © Index Stock Imagery/PhotoLibrary; centre © Corbis;
right © Martin Child/Alamy.
Back cover credits: Left © Getty Images; right © Jon Arnold Images/PhotoLibrary.

C o n t e n t s

KEY TO MAPS

✈   Airport   ⭐ Start of walk/
                                     tour
① 405 Road number   ↘ Cable car
4418m
▲   Mountain   route

Introduction

The 'Golden State' of California is one of the best-known areas on earth, if not from personal experience then vicariously through the media and movies. The history is remarkable. In only 150 years, it has grown from a wilderness of desert and mountains to be the world leader in high technology. It has the sixth-largest gross national product in the world, and each year it adds another 600,000 to its population.

'All scenery in California requires distance to give it its highest charm.'
MARK TWAIN, 1872

'. . . the various landscapes of California – Switzerland and Burgundy and Yorkshire and Scotland and Spain.'
ALISTAIR COOKE, 1973

'When a tree takes a notion to grow in California nothing in heaven or on earth will stop it.'
LILLIAN LELAND, 1890

'California is a wonderful place to live – if you're an orange.'
FRED ALLEN

Hollywood Walk of Fame star

THOMAS COOK's CALIFORNIA

California became a popular destination for travellers as soon as Thomas Cook opened up the USA to British travellers. It featured in Cook's first round-the-world tour of 1872–73, and in 1876 the first dedicated tour to California was organised.

Pullman Cars made the 3,000-mile journey on the transcontinental railroad from the eastern ports to Merced. Here passengers transferred to stagecoach to visit Yosemite Valley (which had become one of the world's first National Parks in 1890). Yosemite was explored by stagecoach or on horseback. The train then continued on to San Francisco for sightseeing.

Cook's inaugural 1876 expedition included all the elements of a present-day tour – right down to tours of Napa Valley vineyards. Only Los Angeles, which began to grow in the 1880s, and Disneyland, which came much later, were not included.

California poppies in spring, Mount Diablo State Park

'Southern California, I found, is a veritable paradise of statuspheres.'
TOM WOLFE

'California, more than any other part of the Union, is a country by itself, and San Francisco a capital.'
JAMES BRYCE, 1901

'I attended a dinner the other morning given for the Old Settlers of California. No one was allowed to attend unless he had been in the State two and one-half years.'
WILL ROGERS, 1924

'The coldest winter I ever spent was a summer in San Francisco.'
MARK TWAIN

'The attraction and superiority of California are in its days. It has better days, and more of them, than any other county.'
RW EMERSON, 1871

'East is East, and West is San Francisco ... Californians are a race of people; they are not merely inhabitants of a state.'
O HENRY, 1910

The land

In many ways California is more like a country than a state. It is big. Of the 50 united states only Alaska and Texas are bigger. The coastline stretches for 2,036km (1,265 miles) from the mist-shrouded redwood forests on the Oregon border to the hot, dry deserts of Mexico, and it is the most fertile state in the Union. Yet, in spite of its size, most of the 37 million population choose life on the geological fault line, or more accurately on a series of fault lines, extending along the whole coastal region, including the infamous San Andreas Fault that passes through San Francisco.

Jumbo Rocks at sunset, Joshua Tree National Park

California is still a landscape under construction and its situation on the junction of two tectonic plates has resulted in some of the most dramatic and contrasting scenery in North America. At 4,418m (14,495ft), Mount Whitney is the highest mountain outside Alaska and is a mere 145km (90 miles) from Bad Water which, at 86m (282ft) below sea level, is the lowest elevation in the western hemisphere. California has three mountain ranges, three desert

systems, thousands of lakes, and forests where you can find not only the tallest trees in the world but also some of the oldest and the largest.

California can conveniently be divided in two, with San Francisco as the hub for northern California and Los Angeles for the southern part of the state. The majority of visitors will fly into one of these hub cities.

The most northerly part of the state, bordering Oregon, is a wilderness of lakes and forests. For the fisherman, hunter, birdwatcher or hiker there is enough territory to explore to last a lifetime. On the northern coast, giant redwoods have been the basis of a timber industry that has provided the main economy for the region.

Further inland, the seismic nature of the state is dramatically evidenced in the moon-like landscape of Lava Beds National Monument and the two volcanoes that are at the end of the chain that includes Mount St Helens in Washington. Mount Shasta, with its five permanent glaciers, rises to 4,319m (14,170ft) above the lake of the same name. The southernmost link in the chain is 3,188m (10,460ft) Lassen Peak, which had its last major eruption in 1915 and now forms the basis of Lassen National Park.

On the eastern border of the state with Nevada at 1,829m (6,000ft) above sea level lies Lake Tahoe, covering an area of 518sq km (200 square miles) and surrounded by the mountains of the Sierra Nevada. Every winter, this is the centre for Olympic-class skiing at resorts such as Squaw Valley. In the summer it transforms into a hikers' paradise.

The Sierra Nevada mountains stretch 644km (400 miles) south from Tahoe. They were created 10 million years ago after the oceanic plate began undercutting the continental plate to form California. Two million years ago glaciers carved out the valleys and granite domes for which the Sierra is famous. Apart from being the highest mountain range in continental United States, it is one of the fastest growing on earth, rising at a rate of 5cm (2in) a year.

The Sierra Nevada forms the eastern boundary of the Central Valley, which is one of the most fertile and productive agricultural areas of the nation. Long, dry summers and wet winters, together with rich alluvial soil that supports everything from cotton to grapes, make the valley ideal for large-scale crop farming.

San Francisco Bay is one of the best natural ports in America and the largest natural harbour on the West Coast. Fed by 16 rivers, it covers 1,036sq km (400 square miles) and joins the sea at the 5km (3-mile) long strait of the Golden Gate. The Bay is actually a drowned river valley – the waters are 97m (318ft) deep beneath the Golden Gate Bridge but go down to a depth of only 30m (100ft) under the eastern section of the Bay Bridge.

The coastal area from the city of San Francisco down to San Diego is the most heavily populated part of the state and boasts one of the most ethnically diverse communities in the United States.

North of San Francisco down as far as Santa Barbara in the south, Sonoma and Napa have the perfect combination of soil type and climate to produce some of the world's best wines.

Southern California is dominated by the Los Angeles conurbation with a 10 million population. Urban sprawl and freeways extend from Santa Monica down as far as Newport Beach and inland to San Bernardino, an area bigger than some East Coast states. The coastal highway continues south to San Diego, California's first settlement and now its second-largest city, with a population of 1,266,700. Driving on beyond San Diego you enter Mexico.

To the east of all this urban development is desert. The desert starts where the Sierra Nevada mountains and the Central Valley end and continues down into Mexico and across to Arizona and New Mexico. Three great desert systems, the Mojave, Colorado and Great Basin, combine to form part of the world's third-largest arid region. This is the land of the cactus and sage brush, sand dunes, and some of the highest recorded temperatures on earth – in Death Valley, a shade temperature of 57°C (134°F) has been recorded!

History

18,000 BC–AD 1500	Migrants from Asia cross the Bering Strait and populate the Americas. By the 16th century California is inhabited by 105 native American tribes speaking more than 100 dialects.
1542	Juan Rodríguez Cabrillo discovers San Diego Bay while on an expedition to the north looking for gold and spices.
1579	Francis Drake, before his knighthood, reputedly lands to the north of San Francisco in the *Golden Hind* and claims the territory for England, naming it Nova Albion.
1769	Father Junípero Serra and Juan Gaspar de Portolá establish the first permanent European settlement in San Diego. El Camino Real is built along the route of present-day Highway 101.
1775	The first ship sails into San Francisco Bay. Within a year the Spanish have founded the Presidio (Fort).
1776	Mission Dolores, the first settlement of San Francisco, is established by the Franciscans. The same year Juan Bautista de Anza reaches San Francisco at the head of the Mexican overland expedition.
1781	Spanish families establish Los Angeles with 41 settlers.
1812	Russians build a trading post at Fort Ross near Bodega Bay.
1821	Mexico attains independence from Spain.
1822	California declares allegiance to the newly independent Mexico.
1826	Overland arrival of Jedediah Smith from across the Sierra Nevada signals the beginning of the US migration westward.
1846	US settlers attempt the unsuccessful 'Bear Flag Revolt'.
1848	Mexico cedes California to the US following the Mexican-American war. James Marshall discovers

	gold while constructing a saw mill by the American River.
1849	Gold rush increases population of San Francisco to 24,000.
1850	California becomes the 31st state of the Union, with its capital at San Jose.
1854	Sacramento becomes the fourth and final capital of the state.
1869	First transcontinental link between the east and west coasts established with the linking of Central Pacific and Union Pacific railroads.
1873	First cable cars run in San Francisco.
1890	Congress establishes Yosemite National Park.
1906	The great earthquake and fire in San Francisco. First film studio opens in Los Angeles.
1920	Population of Los Angeles overtakes San Francisco at 576,673.
1930	Dust Bowl refugees arrive from the Midwest.
1932	Olympic Games held in Los Angeles.
1936–7	The Bay Bridge and the Golden Gate Bridge open.
1945	The original UN Charter is signed in the War Memorial Opera House in San Francisco.
1955	Disneyland opens in Anaheim.
1967	Ronald Reagan elected as Governor.
1984	Olympic Games held in Los Angeles.
1989	Worst earthquake in San Francisco since 1906.
1992	Riots in Los Angeles.
1993	Major earthquake disrupts Los Angeles.
1995	San Francisco 49ers win their 5th Superbowl.
2001	Dot com boom collapses.
2003	Arnold Schwarzenegger is elected governor.
2006	Los Angeles and San Francisco both launch bids to host the 2016 Olympic Games.

Governance

In California, politics has become a struggle not of men but of forces. Once seen as an abundant and promised land, the Golden State in recent years has come up against severe limits. Drought, runaway growth, economic deficits, pollution and a host of other factors have combined to push the state up against the wall. Yet there remains in Californian politics a dream that fuels life here on the edge of the continent, and gives birth to the trends and tastes of America.

California State Capitol building, Sacramento

The main political battleground is the state capital of Sacramento. As a centre of government in the United States, Sacramento is second only to Washington, DC. It is the training ground of US congressmen, presidents and Supreme Court justices, in addition to being the home of innovative government policy.

California also plays a crucial role in national politics. The state sends more legislators to the US House of Representatives and the US Senate than any other. It is the biggest prize in presidential elections as well, giving the winner 54 electoral votes – 20 per cent of the total electoral votes needed to win a presidential election.

Despite California's liberal reputation, it has elected a succession of conservative Republican governors including, of course, Ronald Reagan. In recent years, the state has seen both environmental and especially economic problems grow to gigantic proportions. The responsibility for finding solutions to the state's many problems has now changed hands. In 2002 the incumbent governor, Democrat Gray Davis, was re-elected in a close race against the Republican opponent but was replaced after a recall by Republican Arnold Schwarzenegger.

Welfare reform
California, like America, faces a government deficit growing at an alarming rate. Drastic measures are being sought to bring this runaway fiscal situation under control. Naturally, debate is heated between the conservative Republicans and the more liberal Democrats.

Growth management
Statewide plans are being prepared to control the relentless sprawl of suburban development that is gobbling up land in California's Central Valley, and on the outskirts of Los Angeles, San Francisco and Sacramento. One of the nation's first growth management plans was in San Diego during Pete Wilson's term as mayor.

Environmental issues

In the Los Angeles Basin, 8 million vehicles along with manufacturing plants help to produce the nation's dirtiest air. In the Sacramento River Delta, water diversions have damaged one of the West Coast's most important estuaries and have pushed several species perilously close to extinction.

Along California's north coast, a 'timber war' has broken out between environmentalists and timber companies over the cutting of some of the state's last remaining redwood trees. These and other issues will dominate politics in the state that brought the world Earth Day.

The continued logging of decreasing redwood reserves is an environmental issue that Californians are passionate about

Changing demographics

To drive California's streets is to see America's ethnic future. People from every nation in the world populate its towns and cities. This rich multicultural mix, however, is a mixed blessing. The state is seeing an exodus of people in their productive years, while more and more immigrants are children. From schools to offices, Californians are struggling to meet the needs of newcomers and keep the state's economy strong. In general, there is a growing dissatisfaction with the direction the state is headed and with the state's leadership.

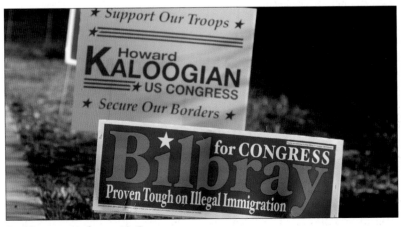

Candidates compete for a seat in Congress

Culture

Of all the states in the nation, none is more culturally diverse than California. Although Sir Francis Drake reputedly landed at Point Reyes in 1579, a few miles north of San Francisco, the first European settlers were the Spanish, who initially explored the southern coast and then moved up from Mexico to establish their chain of missions.

Two young men pose beneath a mural, Mission District, San Francisco

In the mid-1800s a massive influx of European immigrants made their way from the East Coast of the United States in search of gold. This gave a strong European base to the population, which still exists today.

Almost 33 per cent of the population is Hispanic, with the majority of these coming from neighbouring Mexico but also including Cubans, Puerto Ricans and various Central Americans. This figure does not include the thousands of illegal immigrants who continue to cross the Mexican-US border.

The massive Californian agricultural industry could not survive without this tremendous pool of labour. These immigrants, who enter the US daily both legally and illegally, provide low-wage labour, not only for agriculture but in factories and the service industries. They traditionally fill the jobs that other Californians refuse to take.

Behind this new influx of immigrants is an Hispanic establishment whose families have been in California for generations. They are business owners, Congressmen and leaders in local politics throughout the state.

The Hispanic population tends to settle in neighbourhoods. East Los Angeles is 90 per cent Latino and the largest Hispanic community in the US. In San Francisco it is the Mission District. In the Central Valley towns over a third of the population is Hispanic.

Every year on 5 May, Mexican Independence Day, the Latin-American culture throughout California explodes into festivals of song, dance and music that rival Carnival in their exuberance. The Cinco de Mayo celebrations attract over 150,000 participants in San Francisco and San Jose alone.

The oriental influx started as early as 1850 when Chinese railroad workers followed the Gold Rush and started to develop their now world-famous Chinatown in San Francisco. Over the next decade Japanese immigrants began to arrive at Gold Hill, El Dorado County.

In the 1970s California was a major centre for relocating Southeast Asian refugees. By 1980 there were 19 separate Asian groups in the state, the six largest being Chinese, Filipino, Japanese, Asian-Indian, Korean and Vietnamese. Between 1980 and 1990 California's

Asian population almost doubled to 2.3 million people. The latest influx has also been from Southeast Asia and the newcomers are Laotians, Cambodians and Hmong. By the year 2000 Asian-Americans represented about 11 per cent of the population.

California's position as a Pacific Rim trading and banking power has helped to consolidate the state's reputation as an Asian stronghold.

Asians have made their most obvious mark through the multitude of restaurants throughout the state. They generally remain low-key and quietly make their mark without any fuss. Among those who have succeeded in the arts are San Francisco author Amy Tan, who won the 1989 National Book Award, and Stanford graduate David Henry Hwang, who won the Tony Award for his play *M Butterfly*. The black population in California is far less significant than in many eastern states, partially due to the lack of slavery on the West Coast.

The only non-immigrant residents are the Native Americans, and over 1 million make their home in the Golden State – the largest population of any state. They have lived there for over 10,000 years.

California's rich cultural diversity is a major element in the state's charm.

Mexican dancers perform on Olvera Street, Los Angeles

The ethnic diversity of California's population dates back to Gold Rush days when people of every nationality came together to make their fortune. Today, the proximity of Mexico together with the state's strategic position on the Pacific Rim has resulted in significant Latino and Asian populations whose numbers now rival those of Caucasians. Out of 37 million people, half are so-called minorities.

Native American culture is not too obvious in California apart from the ubiquitous Indian casinos that have appeared all over the state. In Palm Springs, the Agua Caliente Band of the Cahuilla Indians owns most of the city and there is an Agua

Caliente Cultural Museum in the Village Green Heritage Center. Pow-wows are occasionally held around Palm Springs but they are too erratic to predict.

Throughout California there are significant communities of immigrants. Chinatown in San Francisco is the largest Chinese settlement outside Asia, Fresno has a large Laotian population, Basques have settled in Bakersfield and in large areas of most of the major cities Spanish is the first language. In most cities there are cultural museums dedicated to these immigrant groups.

This tremendous diversity is most obviously apparent in the variety of ethnic restaurants. Every kind of food is available and usually with a considerable choice of restaurants. This diversity is particularly reflected in the markets, which display an amazing range of produce – from chicken feet to exotic oriental fruit.

Certainly the most colourful manifestation of ethnic pride is in the numerous festivals that occur throughout the year. Chinese New Year and Cinco de Mayo are the big ones that happen in every large town, but don't miss Japanese Cherry Blossom Parade or even the Italian descendants' Columbus Day Parade.

Visiting California is like touring the world without all the travel.

Facing page above: Sudhaswin (L) and Richard Rosenberg (R) meditate with a monk at Thai Buddhist Temple Wat Monkolratanasum, Berkeley; below: man enjoying multicultural Carnival in the Mission District, San Francisco
Above: Middle Eastern dancers on a float celebrating Carnival, Mission District, San Francisco; right: Vietnamese Tet (Vietnamese New Year) lion dance in the streets of San Francisco

Impressions

California is in many ways as familiar as our own backyards. You see it on television, you see it in films, and magazines are always featuring the latest Californian trends. Is this sun-drenched land of milk and honey all that it appears? What is the reality behind the myth?

Tow-away zone parking sign, Los Angeles

Driving

For most visitors the first contact comes after picking up a rental car at the airport. Will the streets be full of budding Steve McQueens screeching round corners at high speed? Far from it. Driving on the right may be confusing and the freeway traffic may appear intimidating but no one goes very fast. All urban freeways have a maximum speed limit of 89km/h (55mph) and most people adhere to this. Generally you can drive at 8km/h (5mph) over the limit without worrying about speeding tickets, but you cannot completely guarantee it.

The most disturbing aspect of freeway travel is that people overtake on all sides. Theoretically there is a fast lane but it is not unusual to find someone in it pottering along at 64km/h (40mph). Fortunately lane discipline is very good, but remember to keep your eyes open and use your mirrors frequently.

Rural freeways have a 105–113km/h (65–70mph) limit. Speed limits will be clearly posted. Speeding tickets are fairly expensive, so take care. Black and white California Highway Patrol cars operate on the freeways, and in towns and cities radar traps are frequently used. Drink-driving laws are extremely tough so do not even take a chance.

Parking

Although, or maybe because, the car is such a major part of life in California, looking for a parking space, particularly in city centres, can be like the search for the Holy Grail.

Street parking is generally regulated by meters with time limits ranging from 15 minutes to 4 hours. The majority of meters allow 1 hour parking and they almost all accept 25 cent coins. Feeding meters is prohibited but it is a common practice nevertheless.

If a meter is obviously broken the usual solution is to write 'Meter Broken' on a paper grocery bag and place it over the meter. This will usually prevent a parking ticket.

Always read notices attached to meters. On major streets in cities parking is often restricted at peak commute times; 7am to 9am and 4pm to 6pm are the most common hours and during this period you will not only get a hefty parking ticket, but also have your car towed at considerable additional expense, not to mention inconvenience.

In business districts some meters will be allocated specifically for commercial vehicles. This will be clearly stated on both the meter and the curb. Parking restrictions are indicated by curb-side colour codes. Red means no parking at any time, day or night. White indicates a drop-off and pick-up zone, usually seen in front of hotels, restaurants and hospitals. Cars cannot be left unattended in this zone. Yellow is strictly for commercial vehicles and is normally only enforced during business hours. The hours will always be posted on the curb. Blue indicates a handicapped zone that is permanently reserved for cars displaying a special handicapped plaque. Certain meters displaying a wheelchair symbol are also exclusively reserved for handicapped motorists. Never ever park in blue zones. They carry the highest parking penalty.

All streets without meters or colour codes are available for parking unless otherwise posted, but remember to always park in the direction of the traffic.

In most towns, parking is prohibited for a couple of hours one day of the week for street cleaning. This can be almost any time of the day or night so make sure you read the small print on street signs.

For more details on Driving *see pp178–9.*

The Bay Bridge with the San Francisco skyline behind

Streets of gold

Many myths have been built on the Californian riches and lifestyle that can seem to be so alluring from the frozen climates of the north. People have been attracted to California in huge numbers since the discovery of gold in 1848. Starting from that onrush, the population has doubled every 20 years.

Spain and Mexico ruled California for almost 80 years without finding the large deposits of gold that they thought existed. Gold was finally discovered in 1848 by James Marshall just days before Mexico transferred California to the United States, which paid $18.25 million for California along with Utah, Nevada, Arizona, New Mexico and even parts of Texas and Colorado. Within ten years, 30 times that amount had been mined from the newly found mines.

California is still a relatively rich state, but the global recession of recent years has certainly had an impact. There is an increasing homeless problem in the big cities and panhandlers begging on street corners are a common sight in all but the most affluent areas.

Food

In one sense California is certainly the land of plenty. The Central Valley is one of the world's most productive agricultural regions and the shelves of any supermarket will reflect the wealth of fresh produce available. An impressive range of fruits and vegetables is grown there and most of them are available year round at inexpensive prices. Grapes are a major crop, and some of the world's finest wines flow from bottles produced in the Napa Valley.

Inevitably a whole culinary trend has grown around this foundation and Californian cuisine has become synonymous with the finest in modern gastronomy. Even in the most modest restaurants the food will generally be good, and certainly plentiful. Service is

Southern California

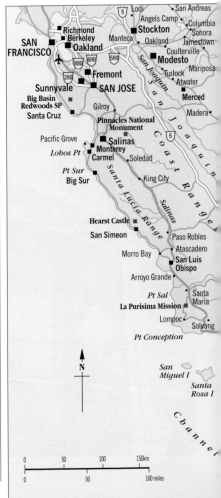

always of a polite and highly efficient level, the expectation of a tip doing much to promote this attitude.

When to go

If you are travelling with children the best months are June, July and August. This is also when Disneyland is at its busiest. If you are looking for a quieter time, March, April, May, late September, October and November are more peaceful. Avoid American holidays when you will be more likely to come across long tailbacks and choked highways.

Northern California

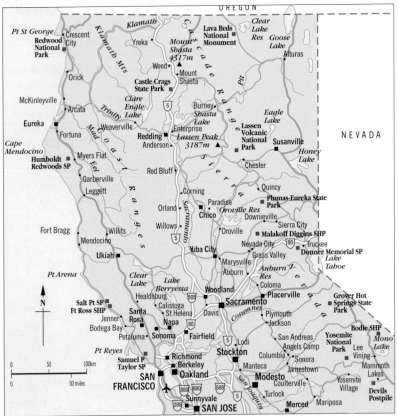

Shopping

Service standards are generally high and there is a strong work ethic. Shops are open late and some shops never close. Most major supermarkets, where you can buy anything from light bulbs to whiskey, are open until at least 10pm and often until midnight. The 7–11 chain of convenience stores never closes at all, 365 days of the year, and they can be found in most towns. They stock a basic range of foodstuffs and also serve coffee and some fast foods.

Even the big department stores open late at least one night a week, and all but the smallest shops are open on Sundays. Sales are a way of life here, and most weeks one store or another will have one. The prices can sometimes be unbelievably low and, depending upon foreign exchange rates, there are some incredible bargains to be found. Local newspapers always carry advertisements with details. Look around; this is California, you will find what you are looking for – and a lot more besides!

Sales tax

Remember that sales tax is always added to the marked price in California. Nothing is more frustrating than waiting in a long queue at a cash register to find that the item you thought you just had enough money to buy has an additional 7 per cent to 8.5 per cent added. The exact rate will depend on the town you are in.

Wet suits required

What about the sun and sand? The beaches are not all golden and sun-drenched. This is not the state to visit for sunbathing. Certainly the weather can be warm, but the Pacific Ocean is definitely not. These are surfing waters and you will see plenty of blond, bronzed surfers wherever waves form, but the bronzed bodies will be well covered in black wet suits to keep out the cold.

Plenty of good sandy beaches can be found, but it is the wild, rocky shores for which California is justifiably famous. From Big Sur up to the Oregon border the Pacific waves crash on to some of the most dramatic shoreline you will ever see. Point Lobos near Monterey has been described as the greatest meeting of land and water on earth.

Seals and sea gulls on Monterey Bay

Dragon head on float, Chinese New Year parade, San Francisco

Water

For all practical purposes the state can be divided into two. Northern California and southern California are as different as chalk and cheese – geographically and politically. The rivalry between the two can be intense and each area has its admirers who will accept no criticism of their chosen land.

The southern half of California is desert. The climate is warm and dry and the insatiable thirst of the giant metropolis of Los Angeles necessitates the diversion of water from the north. The sight of massed lawn sprinklers and gallons of water from washed cars disappearing down the drain is enough to make many northern Californians apoplectic.

For several years water shortage has been a problem throughout California, not just the desert south. Mild winters failed to deliver the snow pack that is needed to provide meltwater to replenish reservoirs. During the most critical periods even restaurants will post notices about only serving water on request, which always seems a bit extreme but indicates the gravity of the situation.

Ethnic evolution

The majority of Californians speak English, but California is the ultimate melting pot of cultures, and each ethnic group has had its impact.

There is a very strong Spanish influence, and the state did in fact start its life as a province of Spanish Mexico. In agricultural areas it is sometimes impossible to find anyone who can understand English. There are towns in the Central Valley where Spanish is the first and only language.

The recent influx of Asians has already created areas in major cities where Asian languages predominate and even shops signs are in Asian scripts. San Francisco's Chinatown is a classic example, where 40,000 Chinese live in a totally Chinese environment. In Los Angeles, a Korean neighbourhood has sprung up in the last few years that is as Korean as areas of Seoul.

California is a state in evolution, a place to test new ideas, a place to live on the cutting edge. It is very difficult to shock the sophisticated Californian.

By any standards California's history is very recent. Any building over 100 years old is of significant importance, and if it is over 150 years old it is as revered as if it were the Tower of London. Where else in the world could you find an archaeological dig on a site dating back to 1917?

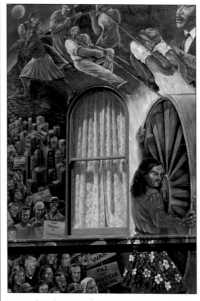

A mural in the Mission district of San Francisco

It's carnival time!

Los Angeles

In LA, as everyone calls it, the car is king. The city is so large that walking is impractical, while public transport is rudimentary at best. Fortunately for the visitor, hiring a car is both simple and cheap, as long as you are 25 or over and hold a valid driving licence.

Los Angeles skyscrapers atop Bunker Hill

A few millimetres on a map can take hours to drive, a problem that is caused as much by traffic as by distance. The distances are indeed impressive. The size of Los Angeles is difficult to comprehend until you have tried to drive from one neighbourhood to another.

From the visitor's perspective, it is impossible to tell where LA begins or ends. Los Angeles County has a population of almost 10 million and covers an area of 10,575sq km (4,083 square miles) with 88 incorporated cities, and the continuous urban sprawl goes way beyond this.

Development stretches from Ventura County in the north to Orange County and Long Beach in the south, and from the Pacific coast across to Riverside County in the east.

This five-county area is bigger than any state excluding California, New York and Texas and houses 16 million people in 88,446sq km (34,149 square miles).

Driving at the speed limit, it takes over two hours to cross the conurbation. However, being able to travel at anything approaching the speed limit is considered a minor miracle. During rush hours there is so much traffic that even the most modest journey can take in excess of two hours.

You could easily spend three weeks in LA and still not have time to do and see everything.

Los Angeles has it all – except for clean air. On rare days during the winter, Santa Ana winds blow away the smog to reveal the San Bernardino mountains forming a spectacular backdrop to the city. On days like this it really becomes the city of angels.

Los Angeles has had much negative media coverage in the last few years, particularly relating to street violence. Although there are probably more problems here than in any other part of California, as one might expect for such a large city, the areas to which visitors are likely to travel are as safe as most cities of the world. Guard against pickpockets, do not leave valuables unprotected, and most problems will be avoided.

The pockets of potential violence are usually far away from the tourist sites. Not visiting Disneyland because of gang wars in Watts is like avoiding Paris because of civil war in Italy.

Beverly Hills

For the mere mortal Beverly Hills is a place to ogle. This super-exclusive independent township, surrounded by Los Angeles, was originally bean fields but soon became the preferred address for Hollywood celebrities.

Elegant mansions can be glimpsed hiding behind security fences and you may even spot the occasional film star, although many of the houses are more likely to be occupied by doctors, lawyers or oil barons.

Film stars Douglas Fairbanks and Mary Pickford built their home, Pickfair, at 1143 Summit Drive, and it quickly became a hangout for the Hollywood set. After Fairbanks' death, Mary Pickford lived there in complete seclusion until her own death in 1980.

The homes of the stars can be found either with the aid of maps on sale at many street corners or more reliably on a bus tour through the town.

A more intimate brush with Hollywood can be had at the sumptuous Beverly Hills Hotel, which was built in 1912. The hotel's legendary Polo Lounge has been, and continues to be, the setting for many a Hollywood deal. If you want to be in films, this is the place to be seen.

Apart from the shopping areas around Rodeo Drive (*see pp148–51*) there are few footpaths in Beverly Hills and walking is frowned upon.

Expect to be questioned by the police if you get out of your Ferrari or Mercedes and they find you wandering aimlessly about.

Night-time skyline and traffic lights on the Hollywood Freeway, Los Angeles

Buena Park

This nondescript town off I-5 in Orange County, a few minutes' drive from Anaheim, used to have several attractions for the visitor. Business has fallen recently, however, and most of these attractions have closed down, though two remain that perfectly complement a visit to Disneyland.

Knott's Berry Farm

Although this was originally exactly what its name implies, Walter Knott started to add attractions to the farm in the 1920s. It is now California's second-biggest tourist enticement, with over 165 rides and attractions covering over 60 hectares (150 acres).

The emphasis of the theme park is on America's past. There is a ghost town, a 19th-century train running around the grounds, a Roaring Twenties area with thrill rides and a penny arcade and Bigfoot Rapids – a very wet ride down California's longest man-made white-water river. If you need even more thrills, Montezooma's Revenge will propel you to 89km/h (55mph) in five seconds both upside down and backwards!

The perfect antidote to all this excitement is the spectacular display of water jets and fountains choreographed to classical music.

8039 Beach Blvd. Tel: (714) 220 5200. www.knotts.com. Open: Sun–Fri 10am– 6pm, Sat 10am–10pm. Admission charge.

Movieland Wax Museum

Over 200 life-size wax models of film and television stars, from Laurel and Hardy to Rambo and Star Trek, inhabit authentic-looking sets. A collection of Hollywood memorabilia completes the exhibit.

If you like exhibits of wax figures, this one is very well done.

7711 Beach Blvd, Buena Park. Tel: (714) 522 1154. www.movielandwaxmuseum.com. Open: Sun–Thur 10am–6pm, Fri & Sat 9am–7pm. Admission charge.

The waterfront at Disneyland, Anaheim

Chinatown

Compared wth San Francisco's, LA's Chinatown is tiny. It is easily seen on foot and consists of the usual array of Chinese restaurants, Chinese groceries and shops selling cheap novelties imported from the Far East.

North Spring Street and North Broadway form the two main thoroughfares, and the **Kong Chow Temple** on the second floor of 931 North Broadway is well worth a visit (*tel: (213) 626 1955*).

Disney's California Adventure

This new attraction adjacent to Disneyland celebrates the state of California, from wineries to Hollywood backlots, although why anyone would want to visit a pretend backlot when a half-hour drive will take you to the real thing is a mystery. However, one attraction almost justifies the entrance fee. 'Soarin' Over California' is the closest you may ever come to feeling like a bird and well worth the inevitable queue.
To check park hours, tel: (714) 999 4565.

Disneyland

California's number one tourist attraction includes seven 'theme' lands extending over 32 hectares (80 acres), while an additional 41 hectares (102 acres) provides parking for 15,167 vehicles! The lands are:

Adventureland – exotic regions of Asia, Africa and the South Pacific.
Critter Country – backwoods setting for Splash Mountain.
Fantasyland – fairytale kingdom.
Frontierland – the world of the pioneers of the Old West.

Main Street USA – small-town America at the turn of the 20th century.
New Orleans Square – home of pirates, ghosts and quaint shops.
Tomorrowland – the world of the future.

A full day is certainly not enough to do justice to Disneyland. Get there early and list priorities with the aid of the map and brochure given at the entrance. Disneyland is open every day of the year, with extended hours during the summer months. Weekends during the summer are the busiest time, when over 9,000 staff are employed! There are always crowds of visitors, but queues at the attractions are generally shorter at the beginning of the week.
43km (27 miles) southeast of Los Angeles Civic Center in Anaheim. To check park hours, tel: (714) 999 4565.
www.disneylandtoday.com

Exposition Park

This 46-hectare (114-acre) park close to downtown LA is the home of the 92,000-seat Los Angeles Memorial Coliseum that was the site of both the 1932 and 1984 Olympic Games. It is also home to three of the city's major museums.

California Science Center

The museum extends through several buildings with exhibits covering subjects as diverse as AIDS and earthquakes. This is very much a hands-on museum and most of the exhibits are interactive.

Next door is the Aerospace Complex, which not only houses a collection of aircraft and spacecraft, but also an IMAX theatre screening the latest spectacles in 70mm surround vision.

Figueroa St at Exposition Blvd. Tel: (323) 724 3623. www.californiasciencecenter.org. Open: daily 10am–5pm. Free admission, but charge for Imax Theatre.

The California African-American Museum

This museum is devoted to black culture and history. It is housed in an airy glass building next to the Aerospace Complex and has new exhibits every few months. *Figueroa St at Exposition Blvd. Tel: (213) 744 7432. www.caamuseum.org. Open: daily 10am–5pm. Admission charge.*

Natural History Museum of Los Angeles County

At the northern end of the park, this is reputedly the most popular museum in Los Angeles. Behind an unimpressive exterior, the Los Angeles County Museum of Natural History houses three floors of galleries which display everything from dioramas of North American and African wildlife to dinosaurs and fossils to cultural exhibits depicting life on the frontier.

There is a particularly good mineral and crystal gallery with a well-guarded room devoted to precious stones. *Tel: (213) 763 3466. www.nhm.org. Open: Mon–Fri 9.30am–5pm, weekends 10am–5pm. Admission charge (free on 1st Tue of each month).*

Farmers' Market

It is doubtful if any farmers actually make it to the market these days, but you will find a wide variety of produce stalls as well as every other type of shop imaginable.

The biggest attractions are numerous snack bars and cafés serving a huge variety of foods, all at affordable prices. *6333 W 3rd St. Tel: (323) 933 9211. www.farmersmarketla.com. Open: Mon–Sat 9am–9pm, Sun 9am–7pm.*

Forest Lawn

Cemeteries may not be a normal tourist attraction, but Forest Lawn on South Glendale Avenue, close to Griffith Park, is said to have in excess of 1 million visitors a year. There you will be able to find the final resting places of stars such as Clark Gable and Jean Harlow.

This perfectly manicured park is also home to larger-than-life-sized reproductions of some of the world's great masterpieces including Michelangelo's *David* and Leonardo da Vinci's *Last Supper* in stained glass.

You can also see the world's largest religious painting on canvas, Jan Styka's *The Crucifixion.*

California Science Center in Exposition Park, Los Angeles

The 121 hectares (300 acres) of lush lawns are a popular, if macabre, picnic site.
1712 South Glendale Ave, Glendale. www.forestlawn.com. Open: daily 9am–5pm. Free admission.

Griffith Park

This 1,619-hectare (4,000-acre) oasis of greenery sits astride the Hollywood Hills. It provides outdoor recreational facilities for the neighbourhood, including an 18-hole golf course, more than 85km (53 miles) of jogging, hiking and bridle trails, and pony rides for youngsters. It is also the home of several important attractions.
Park Ranger Visitor Center, 4730 Crystal Springs Drive. Tel: (323) 665 5188. www.laparks.org/dos/parks/griffithPK/ griffith

Autry National Center

On the northeastern edge of the park, this impressive museum dedicated to the 'Wild West' was opened at the end of 1988. Anyone with even the slightest interest in cowboys will be fascinated by the two floors of exhibits of historic artefacts and Western film memorabilia, such as the jacket worn by Robert Redford as the Sundance Kid or John Wayne's gun belt. Film clips from old Westerns can be seen on monitors throughout the museum.
4700 Western Heritage Way. Tel: (323) 667 2000. www.autrynationalcenter.org. Open: Tue–Sun 10am–5pm. Admission charge.

Griffith Observatory and Planetarium

Although it is doubtful if the telescopes could now penetrate more than a few feet of Los Angeles smog, the observatory is still the major landmark of Griffith Park. On a clear day the views of Hollywood and downtown Los Angeles are spectacular.

The 1930s architecture has provided the backdrop for several Hollywood films, most notably for James Dean in *Rebel Without A Cause*.

The Hall of Sciences has displays on astronomy and meteorology, a planetarium, and a laserium presenting the latest in hi-tech light shows.
2800 East Observatory Rd. Tel: (323) 664 1191. www.griffithobs.org. The observatory will be closed for renovations until late 2006. Call for new opening schedule.

Los Angeles Zoo

The zoo is situated directly opposite the Gene Autry Western Heritage Museum. The 46 hectares (113 acres) opened in 1966 and now house over 2,000 different animals. There is a particularly strong collection of primates and endangered species.
5333 Zoo Drive. Tel: (323) 666 4650. www.lazoo.org. Open: daily 10am–5pm. Admission charge.

Travel Town

Close to the zoo, this transportation museum has a yard full of steam engines and rolling stock as well as examples of just about any other form of transport you can think of. There is a narrow-gauge railway on which children can ride.
4730 Crystal Springs Drive. Tel: (323) 662 5874. www.laparks.org/grifmet/tt. Open: Mon–Fri 10am–4pm, weekends 10am–5pm. Free admission.

The movies

KCET, a Los Angeles public television station, gives technical tours of its studios at 4401 Sunset Boulevard (*tel: (323) 666 6500*). **Burbank Studios** at 4000 Warner Boulevard, Burbank (*tel: (818) 977 8687*), take you behind the scenes to see the daily activities of both **Columbia Pictures** and **Warner Brothers**. Only small groups are accepted, but a thorough introduction to the whole process of film-making is given.

Legend has it that, in 1913, when a downpour of rain greeted Cecil B DeMille in Arizona, he boarded a train and travelled west until he found sunshine. When he did, Hollywood was born.

It all started in an old barn that now houses the **Hollywood Heritage Museum** at 2100 North Highland Avenue (*tel: (323) 874 4005*). The museum is full of memorabilia from the silent movies, including a recreation of DeMille's office.

Today most of the great studios make more films for television than for the cinema, and many of them offer tours.

In Hollywood, **Paramount Studios** at 5555 Melrose Avenue (*tel: (323) 956 1777*) offer a two-hour tour with a historical overview.

Of course, the granddaddy of studio tours is at **Universal Studios**, 100 Universal City Plaza, Universal City (*tel: (800) 711 0080*). Although this is the Hollywood version of Hollywood it is good entertainment value, if not too authentic in other departments.

To feel a part of the scene you may want to pick up a copy of the *Hollywood Reporter* that has covered the industry every weekday morning since 1931.

Statue of the early film maker Burbank

If you really want to get in on the action, the Motion Picture Coordination Office, 6922 Hollywood Boulevard (*tel: (323) 485 5324*), issues a daily shoot sheet giving location details of all films being shot that day.

Hollywood on Location, 8466 Wilshire Boulevard, Beverly Hills (*tel: (661) 250 0080*), offers a more complete service. Every morning

they issue a list of every film and television show being filmed around town. Visitors are supplied with a list of locations, maps, titles and the names of stars they are likely to see. There is a substantial charge for the service.

Facing page above: an artist's view of the special effects used for the filming of the original *King Kong* in the studio
Above: Paramount Pictures gate, Los Angeles
Right: Hollywood stars wall mural, Hollywood

Hollywood

The area was established as a religious agricultural community in 1903, only to become part of Los Angeles in 1910. The intersection of Hollywood and Vine has become synonymous with the glitter and glamour of Hollywood. What a contrast the reality is. This depressingly run-down area is one of the seedier districts of Los Angeles.

Hollywood Boulevard is a must-see area, but the sooner out of it the better. The stars set into the pavement – the so-called Walk of Fame – shine through litter and discarded bottles. What a dubious honour to have your name set in such undignified surroundings!

Mann's (Grauman's) Chinese Theater

Built by Sid Grauman in 1927, and formerly known as Grauman's Chinese Theater, this cinema is one of the essential sights of Hollywood, not so much for the gaudy false Chinese architecture as for the remarkable collection of autographs in cement in front of the theatre, and hand and footprints of film stars such as Cary Grant, Rock Hudson, Doris Day and Joan Crawford. The interior of the theatre is worth a look, with decor equalling the extravagance of the colourful exterior.
6925 Hollywood Blvd. Tel: (323) 464 6266. www.manntheaters.com.
Open: daily noon–midnight.
Admission charge for cinema.

Paramount Studios

Most of the major studios have left Hollywood for the San Fernando Valley, and Paramount Studios is the last of the greats to still occupy their lot on Melrose Avenue. Only recently have members of the public been allowed through their famous gateway, and now behind-the-scenes tours are available.
5555 Melrose Ave. Tel: (323) 956 1777.
www.paramount.com/studio.
Open: weekdays 9am–2pm.
Admission charge, reservations essential.

Hollywood Memorial Park Cemetery

Many of the old Paramount stars are buried here. Among the palm trees and marble statues lie Rudolf Valentino, Peter Finch, Cecil B DeMille, Douglas Fairbanks and many more great Hollywood personalities.
6000 Santa Monica Blvd.

La Brea Tar Pits

These bubbling pits of black goop sit incongruously next to the sleek modern architecture of the LA County Museum of Art on Wilshire Boulevard.

During the Pleistocene period over 200 different types of creatures were trapped in this primordial ooze, and their perfectly preserved skeletons are still being discovered by palaeontologists in one of the richest fossil deposits ever to have been found.

In the adjoining George C Page Museum are displays of many of the discoveries from the Ice Age, including skeletons of mastodons, mammoths and ancient horses. You can also see a working palaeontology laboratory.
5801 Wilshire Blvd. Tel: (323) 857 7243.
www.tarpit.org. Open: Tue–Sun 10am–5pm.
Admission charge (free on 2nd Tue of each month).

Little Tokyo

This enclave of Japanese culture is close to City Hall. There are theatres, Buddhist temples and the two-block Japanese Village Plaza, an outdoor shopping and dining mall.
South San Pedro St.

Long Beach

So far from central Los Angeles that it is difficult to think of it as part of the same county, Long Beach has undergone a facelift in recent years and provides a pleasant break from the big city.

Queen Mary Hotel

The world's once biggest ocean liner lies berthed in the world's largest natural harbour. The refurbished *Queen Mary* was retired to Long Beach where it opened as a hotel, museum and entertainment complex. Daily tours of the ship, including the engine rooms, areoffered to the public, and are free to hotel guests.
Pier J, Long Beach. Tel: (562) 435 3511. www.queenmary.com

Little Italy

The neighbourhood of Naples was developed early last century based on the canal towns of Italy. Quiet waterways are linked by a series of walkways, and what more appropriate way of sightseeing here than by gondola?
Gondola Getaway, 5437 East Ocean Blvd, Long Beach. Tel: (562) 433 9595.

Los Angeles County Museum of Art

This is the largest museum in the West and its exhibits cover the history of art from pre-Columbian gold ornaments to late 20th-century paintings. It is a museum of truly international importance, occupying four main buildings around a central courtyard. The recently added Pavilion for Japanese Art houses the Shin'enkan collection of Japanese paintings and *objets d'art.*

The Ahmanson Building houses an outstanding collection of Indian and Buddhist art, along with collections from Africa, the South Seas, Egypt and some of the great masterpieces of the Renaissance. More great art than in many major museums is housed here. This is an awe-inspiring collection worthy of hours, if not days, of browsing.
5905 Wilshire Blvd. Tel: (323) 857 6000. www.lacma.com. Open: Mon, Tue & Thur noon–8pm, Fri noon–9pm, Sat & Sun 11am–8pm. Admission charge.

Recreating the Pleistocene period, La Brea Tar Pits, Los Angeles

Los Angeles environs

San Gabriel Mountains
Angeles National Forest

Malibu
Getty Center

Perched on a ridge in the Santa Monica mountains, a site perfectly situated to allow visitors a 360-degree view of Los Angeles, the magnificent Getty Center houses a priceless collection of both fine and decorative arts.

The 45-hectare (110-acre) campus houses five pavilions: North, East, South, West and Exhibitions. The art is arranged chronologically, starting in the North (pre-1600) and ending in the West (post-1800). Each Pavilion also has an Educational Area where you can talk to a docent about the exhibitions, interact with multimedia computer stations, and learn more about the art in the adjoining galleries.

The Exhibitions Pavilion houses temporary exhibits.

A number of amenities make your visit both more educational and more enjoyable. This is truly one of the world's great art experiences and deserves a whole day.
1200 Getty Center Drive, off I-405.
Tel: (310) 440 7300. www.getty.edu/visit.
Open: Tue & Wed 11am–7pm, Thur & Fri 11am–9pm, Sat & Sun 10am–6pm.
Free admission.

Marina del Rey

This pleasant seaside neighbourhood lies conveniently close to both Los Angeles International Airport and downtown Los Angeles.

There is not really any sightseeing here, but overlooking the Marina del Rey harbour is Fisherman's Village. Its colourful Cape Cod-style buildings house speciality shops and restaurants which are open daily all year round.

Beach life

The most sought-after houses on the southern coast of California face the beach – no matter that the fog rolls in and the ocean is cold.

The beach plays a major part in the lives of Californians. From Malibu down to Laguna, whatever the weather, on any day of the week, people can be seen using this narrow strip of sand between the land and the sea.

Surfers are always searching for the perfect waves and often find them north of Malibu. Anglers use every structure that juts into the sea to cast their lines. Joggers jog and skateboarders skate.

At Santa Monica and Venice Beach, the weekend brings out a veritable circus of street performers. Jugglers, people on roller skates, weight lifters and fast-food vendors are all out in force competing with each other for the ever-present audience.

Muscle Beach, just to the north of Venice, is a popular place to watch the blond gods of the Pacific coast pumping iron and impressing the girls.

The girls are no less hesitant about impressing the boys, skating along the boardwalks in the skimpiest of bikinis.

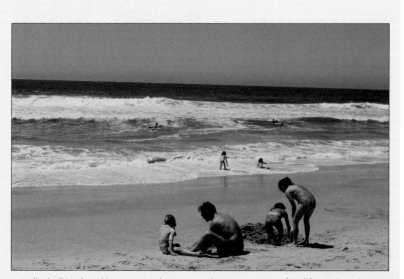

Volleyball is played in earnest wherever there is an open stretch of sand. Hermosa Beach has a televised world volleyball championship every summer.

Not all the beaches are pretty. Huntington Beach has ugly oil derricks along the coast and offshore, and this hunger for offshore oil is a topic of considerable environmental controversy.

In the northern part of the state the beaches are more popular with the rugged outdoor enthusiasts. Here, waves continually crash on to the rocky coastline and cold winds blow in from the Pacific Ocean. It may be the sunny state of California but this northern coast has a true northern climate.

Facing page above: Surfers at dawn near the Huntington Beach Pier, Huntington Beach; below: Fun at dusk along the Newport Beach Pier
Above: Weekend on the beach at Carlsbad near San Diego; below: Working out at the Muscle Beach Gym, Venice Beach

Pasadena City Hall exterior

Museum of Contemporary Art (MOCA)

It may be surprising that what must surely be one of the trendiest cities on earth did not have a museum devoted exclusively to contemporary art until 1986.

It had been hoped to open the new museum in time for the 1984 Olympics, but when this was obviously not going to happen, a temporary gallery was opened that proved to be so popular that it is still in use. The Temporary Contemporary, as it is called, is located at 152 North Central Avenue, and a free shuttle service operates between the museum and the temporary gallery.

The museum has a small permanent collection of works from the major modern movements, particularly artists that have worked in California such as Mark Rothko and Clyfford Still. It also regularly features travelling exhibits.

The museum as a building is worth seeing in itself. The red sandstone and glass building was designed by Japanese architect Arata Isozaki.
250 South Grand Ave, Los Angeles. Tel: (213) 626 6222. www.moca.org. Open: Tue, Wed, Fri & weekends 11am–5pm, Thur 11am–8pm. Admission charge (free on Thur 5–8pm).

Music Center

Three performance spaces are combined into this impressive complex: the Dorothy Chandler Pavilion, which is home to the Civic Light Opera and the Los Angeles Philharmonic Orchestra; the Mark Taper Forum, a theatre for contemporary drama; and the Ahmanson Theatre, a 2,000-seat auditorium for traditional drama.
135 North Grand Ave. Tel: (213) 972 7211. www.musiccenter.org. Free tours are offered in English, Spanish and French. Call for information.

NBC Studios

Most of the major film and television studios have relocated to Burbank in the San Fernando Valley. NBC no longer gives public tours of the studios, but free TV show tickets are available and must be requested two weeks in advance.
3000 West Alameda Ave, Burbank. Tel: (818) 840 3537. www.seeing-stars.com/StudioTours/NBCtour

Old Town

Close to the heart of modern Los Angeles there still remains a block of buildings dating back to the birth of the city. The **Pueblo de Los Angeles State Historic Park** preserves this historic area that was first settled in 1781.

The 1818 Avila Adobe is the oldest building in Los Angeles. It is open to the public. The other buildings line either side of Olvera Street, a pedestrianised way that is a permanent Mexican marketplace with craft shops and cafés almost obscuring the historic buildings behind. It gives a strong flavour of early Spanish California.

El Pueblo de Los Angeles Historic Park, 845 North Alemeda St. Tel: (213) 485 8372. www.cityofla.org/ELP/. Free walking tours start at 130 Paseo de la Rosa Tue–Sat on the hour, 10am–1pm. Shops open weekdays until 8pm.

Pasadena

Pasadena came to prominence in the late 1900s because of its agreeable climate. Only 20 minutes by freeway from downtown Los Angeles, the town sits at the foot of the San Gabriel Mountains.

Driving around the town will give a good impression of past and present wealth, with many very fine houses on tree-lined avenues.

The historic centre of the town has been restored over the last few years and, in a 10-block area known as 'Old Town', pawn shops and adult book stores are gradually giving way to art galleries and trendy restaurants. Fortunately the original Victorian façades are being preserved.

Huntington Library and Art Gallery

It would be difficult to find a more impressive collection of paintings and manuscripts anywhere.

Of the four million items in the library, several are of unique value. The Ellesmere Manuscript of Chaucer's *Canterbury Tales* dates back to 1410. There is a two-volume Gutenberg Bible printed on parchment in 1455, a Shakespeare Folio edition and Audubon's original edition of *Birds of America*. The collection of American art is impressive, but you will also find Gainsborough's *Blue Boy* and Thomas Lawrence's *Pinkie* among the paintings.

As if all this is not enough, the grounds of the Huntington match the galleries in interest, with several different gardens, each devoted to a different theme. The Japanese Garden is the most popular, but there is also a herb garden, rose garden, subtropical garden and a Shakespeare garden with only plants that existed in the playwright's time. There are guided tours through the gardens every day at 1pm.

The 3½-hour opening time is unrealistic to do justice to this collection and it is worth getting there early. Sundays can be very crowded.

1151 Oxford Rd, San Marino. Tel: (626) 405 2100. www.huntington.org. Open: Tue–Fri 1–4.30pm, Sat & Sun 10.30am–4.30pm. Admission charge.

Norton Simon Museum of Art

This unusual modern group of buildings houses a collection of art spanning 2,500 years. It is an impressive collection with paintings by Rembrandt, Raphael and Rubens; drawings by Goya; sculpture by Rodin and Moore; and works by Cézanne, Van Gogh and Degas.

The biggest display is of French art, from Poussin and Watteau through to the Impressionists and on to the Cubists, with important works by most of the major artists of each movement. One gallery is devoted to 88 works by Degas, and the museum has countless models for his bronze figures.

411 West Colorado Blvd, Pasadena. Tel: (818) 449 6840. www.nortonsimon.org. Open: Thur–Sun noon–6pm. Admission charge.

Dinosaur topiary on the Third Street Promenade, Santa Monica

Santa Monica

Santa Monica is a beach town with one of the best piers in California as its focus.

Here you will find the California of the Beach Boys, bronzed surfers, body-builders working out, and every kind of performer and musician. On the beach, just by the pier, volleyball courts are in constant use, even late into the night.

The pier itself has a multitude of shops, a couple of restaurants, an early 20th-century roundabout with hand-painted horses that were featured in *The Sting*, more modern dodgem cars, shooting galleries, pinball arcades and all manner of Californian characters to complete the scene.

It is worth spending an hour or two strolling around the beach and pier to get the flavour of laid-back southern California.

Southwest Museum

The native American Indians are the subject of this museum housed in a mission-style building high above downtown Los Angeles.

A good collection of jewellery, basketwork and weaving by the Pueblo Indian tribes forms the core of the collection, but the focus is now on all Native Americans, rather than just those from the southwest as the museum's name implies.

234 Museum Drive, Los Angeles.
Tel: (323) 221 2163.
www.southwestmuseum.org.
Open: Tue–Sun 10am–5pm.
Admission charge.

Universal Studios

A tour of Universal Studios should be very high on the list of every first-time visitor to Los Angeles.

This is as close to 'Hollywood' as most

people will ever get. It is, however, a Hollywood version of 'Tinsel Town'.

The half-day tour takes you through the backlots covering 170 hectares (420 acres) with 36 sound stages and over 10,000 film-makers. Many of the scenes on the tour are instantly recognisable by film buffs: the *Psycho* house, streets of façades used for any number of Westerns, the 1920s street that was the location for *The Sting* – they are all here.

Just as interesting as this behind-the-scenes experience are the special attractions, which are the most memorable. Where else is it possible to experience the full magnitude of an 8.3 earthquake while on an underground train with water mains bursting all around, and still live to tell the tale?

The effects are quite incredible, and just from the engineering point of view they are well worth the admission fee. Within an hour the visitor will have an encounter with King Kong, be attacked by Jaws, and witness a parting of the Red Sea, before being on the verge of getting washed away by a flash flood.

After the tour there is a choice of several different shows, including thrill ride *Revenge of the Mummy,* action spectacular *Waterworld* and *Van Helsing: Fortress Dracula*, or you can wander around The Streets of the World which is like one huge film set.
100 Universal City Plaza, Universal City. Hollywood Freeway, exit Linkershim Blvd. Tel: (818) 622 3801. www.themeparks.universalstudios.com. Open: Mon–Fri 9am–5pm in the summer, 10am–3.30pm rest of the year; Sat & Sun 9.30am–3.30pm. Admission charge.

Venice

The best way to describe Venice is funky. Walking along the boardwalk you will be passed by just about every form of pedestrian-powered wheeled transport in existence – roller skates, bicycles, monocycles, skateboards, along with the usual array of joggers and surfers on their way to 'catch the big one'.

In the summer the beach is packed with sun worshippers and the parking problem becomes a nightmare.

At all times of year there is plenty of activity. Up near 18th Avenue is Muscle Beach where aspiring Arnold Schwarzeneggers can be watched pumping iron, while at the southern end of town is a 335m (1,100ft) long pier.

Only three blocks away from all this activity is the small area of tranquil canals that gave Venice its name (*see p42*).

The stuff that dreams are made of: pose with a Marilyn Monroe lookalike at Universal Studios Hollywood Resort

Walk: the Venice canals

This is the only area of Venice's canals that has been preserved. This quiet, residential neighbourhood is a peaceful relief from the frenetic activity of Venice Beach. *Allow 1½ hours.*

From Los Angeles take the Santa Monica Freeway (I-10) west to Venice Boulevard. Follow Venice Boulevard west to the ocean. South Venice Boulevard leads to a car park on the sea front. During the summer this fills very early, but there are other car parks in the area.

Walk back from the car park on the right-hand side of the street for three blocks until you pass over a small bridge crossing the Grand Canal. Steps lead down to a footpath that runs along the length of the canal.

Cigarette manufacturer Abbot Kinney had a dream of creating a Venice of America. Twenty six kilometres (16 miles) of canals were dredged from the Santa Monica Bay swamps in 1905, but the discovery of oil spelled doom. The canals became polluted and by 1929 the city had most of them filled in. This one section of the Grand Canal remains. *Walk along the bank to the far end, past the back gardens of an assortment of cottages. Fortunately the snarling dogs that seem to be everywhere never materialise and remain safely behind fences. On your left you will pass four canals running at right angles to the Grand Canal. Cross the bridge over the Sherman Canal, the last of the four, and just meander back along the footpaths and enjoy this oasis of tranquillity in the heart of Los Angeles.*

The houses that back on to the canals are an interesting architectural mix from modest cottages to mini-palazzos. Too expensive for the far-out, bohemian fringe of Los Angeles, they attract latter-day yuppies with artistic inclinations.

The attraction of this area is obvious as you stroll along the footpaths. Where else in this giant metropolis can you find the quiet, European atmosphere provided by this early 20th-century dream?

Dell Avenue cuts through the canal area and this will take you straight back to South Venice Boulevard whenever you are ready.

Take along some bread to feed the ducks and other waterfowl that have made these canals their home.

The Venice boardwalk has several fast-food vendors. All the way along Ocean Front Walk you will be able to find every kind of junk food known to the human race. The quintessential Venice restaurant is the Sidewalk Café at 1401 Ocean Front Walk (*tel: (310) 392 4687*), about a 10-minute walk north from Venice Boulevard, where breakfast, lunch and dinner are served. Here you

Bridge over Venice Canal, Los Angeles

can sit on the boardwalk and enjoy the free entertainment provided by the usual assortment of Venice *habitués* passing to and fro.

Houses along one of the few surviving canals in Venice, Los Angeles

San Diego

San Diego is the ideal vacation destination. The climate is superb, with warm, sunny days which the Pacific breezes prevent from getting too hot. It rarely rains (a problem for residents but not for visitors), it never freezes, and the average annual daytime temperature range is between 14°C (58°F) and 21°C (70°F). It has 113km (70 miles) of sandy beaches and plenty of attractions, including what is considered to be the world's finest zoo and an enormous natural harbour, and it is a cultural centre of some significance.

Casa do Prado building, Balboa Park, San Diego

Most of the two-and-a-half million residents of San Diego County live within 48km (30 miles) of the ocean, and the sea plays a major role in everyday life. This is the headquarters of the 11th Naval District and provides a home for one of the world's largest fleets of fighting ships. It is also home for the America's Cup, the prestigious sailing trophy.

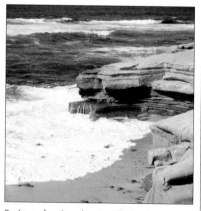

Rocks, surf and sand on La Jolla Beach, near San Diego .

There is history too. This is the birthplace of California. Father Junípero Serra established his first mission here in 1769 but over 200 years before that the Portugese explorer Juan Rodríguez Cabrillo landed in what is now San Diego Bay and claimed it for Spain. The 'Old Town' has been made into a State Historic Park.

Just 32km (20 miles) from downtown San Diego and you are in Tijuana across the border – but remember to take your passport, and non-US citizens will need to produce a multiple entry visa.

In spite of being the sixth-largest city in the United States and California's second-biggest city, with a population of over one million, there never seems to be the pressure of time that occurs in Los Angeles. The international airport must be one of the most convenient in the world, being situated only three miles from the heart of the city. Downtown hotels can be reached within minutes of leaving the airport.

San Diego

**Upper map labels:**

Salk Institute
Scripps Aquarium
University of California
Miramar Naval Air Station
0 5km
0 3 miles
Point La Jolla
La Jolla Caves
University City
LA JOLLA
La Jolla Museum of Contemporary Art
San Clemente Canyon
SANTEE
Soledad Natural Park
North Clairemont
Tierrasanta
San Diego
Montgomery Field
PACIFIC BEACH
CLAIREMONT
274
Serra Mesa
EL CAJON
Grantville
Lake Murray
MISSION BEACH
Mission Bay Park
LINDA VISTA
Tecolote Canyon Natural Park
Mission San Diego de Alcala
LA MESA
University of San Diego
Sea World
Mission Valley
San Diego Jack Murphy Stadium
Alvarado Canyon
Aztec Bowl
San Diego Railroad Museum
Ocean Beach
OCEAN BEACH FREEWAY
Midway
Old Town
163
Balboa Park
San Diego Zoo
Museums
SAN DIEGO
Chollas Park
Sunset Cliffs Park
209
San Diego Int Airport
805
LEMON GROVE
POINT LOMA
San Diego Bay
Maritime Museum
MONTGOMERY FREEWAY
Encanto
94
North Island U.S. Naval Air Station
CORONADO BAY BRIDGE
CORONADO
San Diego Bay
JACOB DEKEMA FREEWAY
NATIONAL CITY
Sweetwater Reservoir
Cabrillo National Monument
75
Lincoln Acres
54
Sunnyside
Sweetwater Park
N

Lower map (SAN DIEGO DOWNTOWN) labels:

San Diego International Airport
SAN DIEGO FREEWAY
163
Balboa Park (Museums)
PERSHING DRIVE
San Diego Bay
N
1ST AVENUE
4TH AVENUE
6TH AVENUE
CABRILLO FREEWAY
PARK BLVD
U.S. Naval Hospital
Firehouse Museum
5
Maritime Museum
ASH STREET
ASH STREET
Balboa Stadium
Cruise Ship Terminal
HARBOR DRIVE
PACIFIC HIGHWAY
KETTNER BOULEVARD
STATE AVENUE
Courthouse
Convention & Performing Arts Center
Copley Symphony Hall
C STREET
BROADWAY
Broadway Pier
BROADWAY
25TH
Navy Pier
Federal Buildings
Horton Plaza
6TH AVENUE
10TH
11TH AVENUE
12TH AVENUE
16TH
SAN DIEGO FREEWAY
MLK JR FRWY
94
Tuna Harbor
MARKET STREET
MARKET STREET
SAN DIEGO DOWNTOWN
0 400 800m
Seaport Village
HARBOR DRIVE
Gaslamp Quarter
Embarcadero Marine Park
Villa Montezuma
Jesse Shepard House

Balboa Park
See also p48.

Botanical Building
Right in the centre of the park, behind the lily pond, is a building that looks like a huge overturned basket. In fact, the steel framework was made for a station belonging to the Santa Fe Railroad, but was purchased for the 1915 Exposition.

It now houses a collection of ferns and other tropical/subtropical plants.
Tel: (619) 236 5717.
Open: daily, except Fri, 10am–4pm.

California Tower
This 61m (200ft) high landmark structure was the centrepiece for the 1915 Panama-California Exposition. Its Spanish Renaissance architecture still dominates the main thoroughfare of Balboa Park. Immediately below it is the Museum of Man.

The tower houses a 100-bell carillon that chimes every quarter-hour.

Museum of Photographic Arts
The museum is one of the few in North America devoted just to photography. A small gallery has regular exhibitions of prints by major photographers, and an excellent shop has a wide range of publications on photography.
Tel: (619) 238 7559. www.mopa.org.
Open: daily 10am–5pm, Thur until 9pm.
Admission charge.

Old Globe Theater
The San Diego Repertory Company makes its home in this recreation of Shakespeare's original Globe Theatre in London. It was originally built for the 1935 California-Pacific International Exhibition, burned down in 1978, and was reconstructed, winning a coveted Tony Award for its stage.

Adjoining the Globe are the **Lowell Davies Festival Theater** and the **Simon Edison Center for the Performing Arts**
Tel: (619) 239 2255.
www.TheOldGlobe.org.

Reuben H Fleet Space Theater and Science Center
The Space Theater is California's only Omnimax theatre, presenting spectacular films on a hemispherical screen that envelopes the audience, making them feel part of the action. State-of-the-art sound is delivered by 152 separate speakers. It also features one of the largest planetariums in the country.

The Science Center is a hands-on exhibit, essentially for children, covering the laws of science.
Tel: (619) 238 1233. www.rhfleet.org.
Open: daily 9am–9pm.
Admission charge.

San Diego Air & Space Museum
The whole history of aviation is covered in this circular building, from a replica of the *Spirit of St Louis* to the latest spacecraft and everything in between, including modern fighter aircraft in the centre courtyard of the museum.

There are over 70 aircraft, spacecraft and associated artefacts in the collection. The exhibits unfold in a chronological fashion, starting with the Montgolfier brothers' hot-air balloon and ending with America's current Space Shuttle programme. Every aspect of aviation is covered, including an exhibit on women's role in aviation.

Alongside the main exhibits is the **International Aerospace Hall of Fame**. The Hall of Fame concept is popular throughout the US, and in this museum it is nothing more than a collection of annotated photographs of the great men and women in the history of aerospace. *2001 Pan American Plaza. Tel: (619) 234 8291. www.aerospacemuseum.org. Open: daily 10am–4.30pm. Admission charge.*

San Diego Automotive Museum

Situated next door to the Aerospace Museum, this museum has a display of over 80 vehicles including horseless carriages, brass cars, performance and exotic cars, and future prototypes. *2080 Pan American Plaza. Tel: (619) 231 2886. www.sdautomuseum.org. Open: daily 10am–5pm. Admission charge.*

San Diego Model Railroad Museum

In the basement of the same building as the Museum of Photographic Arts you can discover the world's largest collection of mini-gauge trains.

Scenes of San Diego and southern California have been reduced to scale to provide a landscape for the trains. *Tel: (619) 696 0199. www.sd-mrm.org. Open: Wed–Fri 11am–4pm, Sat & Sun 11am–5pm. Admission charge.*

San Diego Museum of Art

Although this is not one of the great art museums of the world, there is a good collection that is particularly strong on Flemish and pre-Renaissance painting.

Adjoining the museum is a sculpture garden with a small but excellent collection by artists such as Calder, Miró, Hepworth and Moore.

As with many of the buildings in Balboa Park, the architecture is as interesting as the exhibits. The façade of the Museum of Art is a copy of the 17th-century University of Salamanca in Spain. *Tel: (619) 232 7931. www.sdmart.org. Open: Tue–Sun 10am–6pm. Admission charge.*

San Diego Museum of Man

At the core of the collection are artefacts from the Pueblo Indians of the southwest and the Aztec and Mayan settlements of Latin America by the Smithsonian Institution in Washington, DC.

There is now a broader anthropological base to the museum, highlighting humankind's physical and cultural development. In addition, there are frequent special exhibits from Pacific Rim cultures. *Tel: (619) 239 2001. www.museumofman.org. Open: daily 10am–4.30pm. Admission charge.*

San Diego Natural History Museum

The environment of southern California is the main emphasis of this 100-year-old institution. There are the usual dioramas of the Californian coast and a topical exhibit called 'On the Edge', which focuses on rare and endangered plants and animals.

As with many of the museums in Balboa Park, the building is almost more impressive than its contents. *Tel: (619) 232 3821. www.sdnhm.org. Open: daily 10am–4.30pm. Admission charge.*

Walk: Balboa Park

Close to the centre of San Diego, Balboa Park has a higher concentration of cultural attractions than anywhere in California. In addition to the world-famous zoo there are 14 different museums and an arts and crafts market.
Allow 2 hours, excluding museum visits.

From downtown San Diego take I-5 north to the Pershing Drive exit, and follow the signs to the zoo. Ample parking is available but carefully note where you left your car – the car park is vast!

1 San Diego Zoo
The world's biggest zoo deserves a day to itself. It first opened as part of the 1915 Panama-California Exposition and became one of the first zoos to take animals out of cages and put them into

a natural environment.
The walk starts by the main entrance to the zoo and follows the signs to Balboa Park. After leaving Zoo Place you will pass a 48-seat miniature railroad on your left.

2 Spanish Village Art Center
Immediately on your left you will see a collection of low, Spanish-style buildings. This arts and crafts complex houses the studios of 42 woodcarvers, potters,

painters, sculptors, photographers and silversmiths, whom you can watch at work and, of course, buy the works they produce. The Center was originally built as part of the 1935–6 California-Pacific Exhibition (*open: daily 11am–4pm*).
Cross the Village Place and pass between the San Diego Natural History Museum on your left and the Spanish Baroque Casa del Prado on your right. Continue to El Prado and turn left.

3 Balboa Plaza

This is the end of El Prado. The Inez Grant Parker Memorial Rose Garden will be behind you as you look down El Prado to the landmark California Tower. You can reach the garden across the footbridge over Park Boulevard. It is an All-American Rose Selection Display Garden. Next to the Rose Garden is the Desert Garden with a wide variety of succulents indigenous to the desert.
Walk down El Prado between the ornate Spanish–Mexican-style buildings towards the California Tower.

4 The Lily Pond

During World War II this was used as a swimming pool for patients at the US naval hospital. The steel-frame structure behind the pond is the Botanical Building containing over 500 species of tropical and subtropical plants.
Continue down El Prado towards the California Tower. After passing the Timken Art Gallery on your right, El Prado is open to vehicular traffic. Cross the Plaza de Panama, and on your left on the corner, after joining El Prado, is the San Diego Art Institute. Walk along the

porticoes adjoining it and in an enclosed courtyard to the side is the Alcazar Garden.

5 The Alcazar Garden

Designed for the 1915 Panama-California Exposition, it is modelled on the gardens of the Alcázar in Seville, Spain, which were destroyed during the Spanish Civil War. It is an ideal hideaway for a quiet picnic.
Return to the Plaza de Panama and turn right.

6 Japanese Friendship Garden

On your left is a traditional Japanese garden adapted to the climate and topography of San Diego. It provides a perfect place for quiet contemplation. Next to the garden is the Spreckels Organ Pavilion (*see p50*), but unless you are in the park on a Sunday at 2pm, the world's biggest organ will be protected behind a 12-ton metal curtain.
Return to the Plaza de Panama, turn right on to El Prado, and retrace your path back to the zoo.

Balboa Park is the ideal place for a picnic, but the Waters Café @ SDMA in the Museum of Art Sculpture Garden (part of the Museum of Art) serves excellent light lunches (*open: Tue–Fri 11am–2.30pm, Sat & Sun 11am–3.30pm*).

A more formal and romantic setting can be found in the Café del Rey Moro behind the Visitor Center. This re-creation of a Moorish palace in Spain has a romantically landscaped terrace, indoor dining and a piano bar (*open: Mon, for lunch only, Tue–Sun, lunch & dinner, tel: (619) 234 8511*).

San Diego Zoo

This is often considered to be the world's greatest zoo, and for very good reasons.

In a time when zoos are falling both out of favour and out of business, San Diego Zoo is a remarkable success. For one thing it is big and covers 52 hectares (128 acres). There is a lot of space for the animals, and there are a lot of animals – 3,900 from 800 species. An effort has been made to concentrate on endangered species and to develop breeding programmes for these animals.

The site of the zoo extends across a steep canyon, and to tour the zoo on foot involves some serious walking. This is certainly the best way to make the most of the exhibits, but for those unable to cope with the steep gradients there is a three-mile double-decker-bus tour through the zoo which also provides an informative commentary.

Yet another aspect of the zoo can be found by taking a trip in the **Skyfari** aerial tram for a bird's-eye view above the treetops.

Some of the world's rarest and most interesting primates are on display here, and a recently opened gorilla exhibit –

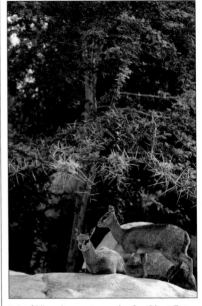

Pair of klipspringers atop rocks, San Diego Zoo

the **Gorilla Tropics** – re-creates over a hectare (2^1/2 acres) of the habitat that is the home for six lowland gorillas.

Also of interest is a rainforest complete with artificial mist, a large collection of koala bears from Australia and tiny pygmy chimpanzees from central Africa.

Tel: (619) 231 1515. www.sandiegozoo.org. Open: daily 9am–4pm. Admission charge.

Spreckels Organ

Every Sunday at 2pm a recital is given on this giant among organs. It was given to the city in 1915 by the sons of millionaire Adolf Spreckels and remains the biggest open-air organ in the world. The longest pipes are almost 10m (33ft) in length.

San Diego Safari

56km (35 miles) to the north of San Diego off I-15, the San Diego Zoo's Wild Animal Park re-creates both Asian and African habitats on its 728-hectare (1,800-acre) site. Over 2,500 animals roam free as they are viewed from elevated walkways or on a 50-minute tour on the Wgasa Bush Line monorail.

15500 San Pasqual Valley Road, Escondido. Tel: 619 234 6541. Open: daily. Admission charge.

Spanish Village Arts and Crafts Center
Leaving the zoo and entering the Prado area of Balboa Park you will pass a group of low, Spanish-style buildings where craftsmen and artists are busy at work turning out a variety of souvenirs for visitors.

This is very much a commercial venture, but occasionally interesting work can be found here.
Tel: (619) 238 9050.
www.spanishvillageart.com.
Open: daily 11am–4pm.

Coronado

The exclusive community of Coronado is almost an island. A long, narrow sand bar known as the Silver Strand connects it to the mainland. Until 1969 the only access was by ferry or a very long drive, but then the San Diego–Coronado Bay Bridge was built, and now it only takes a few minutes to drive there from downtown San Diego.

Coronado has the ambience of a different era. Although it is now only minutes from the busy centre of San Diego it is like being in a quaint village. The affluence of the community is reflected in the immaculate tree-lined avenues and expensive houses, but, pleasant as it must be to live here, there is not a lot for the visitor to do.

The main attraction is the **Hotel del Coronado.** This is one of the great hotels of the world, built of wood in 1888 and still in use as a luxury hotel. Thomas Edison personally supervised the installation of electricity in the hotel, which at the time was the only building outside New York to be fully served with electricity.

Twelve American presidents have stayed here and it has been made a National Historic Landmark. It was featured in the film *Some Like It Hot* and the management make great play of this, but even without the Hollywood connection the hotel is worth a visit. Wander around the beautifully kept grounds and down to the beach. Unfortunately most of the beach area along the Silver Strand has been used for military manoeuvres, and warning notices make it quite clear that the area is out of bounds.

Botanical Garden building, Balboa Park, San Diego

Gaslamp Quarter

In the 1800s this was San Diego's main street area. At the turn of the 20th century it became a flourishing red-light district. It is in the heart of modern San Diego and, like many inner-city areas, it suffered a long period of neglect.

A concerted effort has been made to restore the district to its original glory and it has been designated a National Historic District. Many of the buildings have now been renovated. The area still has not been able to shake off its somewhat seedy image, but now the pawn shops rub shoulders with trendy new restaurants and antique shops.

There are several very fine examples of Victorian architecture, and the Gaslamp Quarter Foundation at 410 Island Avenue can provide a free, detailed map of the district with histories of the individual buildings. They also offer tours on Saturdays at 11am. A small donation to the foundation is expected.
Broadway to Harbor Drive between 4th & 6th aves. Tel: (619) 233 5227.

Horton Plaza

This colourful, modern shopping plaza that opened in 1985 is the centrepiece for the new downtown area of San Diego. It is a textbook example of good design. The human scale and visually stimulating architecture combine with first-rate

shops to make shopping here a totally satisfying experience. Even if you hate shopping it is still worth walking through the plaza just for the pleasure of the building. How many shopping malls can you say that about?

On the upper level of the plaza is a wide range of restaurants and cafés serving food from all over the world and in every price range. You will also find here a seven-screen cinema and two performing arts theatres.
Broadway and G St.

La Jolla

Residents of this ritzy community of San Diego like to think of their neighbourhood as a separate entity and refer to it as 'The Village'. Even the post office stamps mail La Jolla although it is part of the city of San Diego.

Lamp standard and buildings,
Gaslamp Quarter,
San Diego

GASLAMP
QUARTER

GASLAMP
QUARTER

GASLAMP
QUARTER

GASLAMP
QUARTER

HISTORIC HEART OF SAN DIEGO

HISTORIC HEART OF SAN DIEGO

The dramatic exterior of Horton Plaza, San Diego

La Jolla (pronounced 'La Hoya') is not unlike an exclusive Mediterranean resort with the same mix of expensive houses, exquisite boutiques, gourmet restaurants and grand hotels. The cliff-lined coast adds to this impression.

It is the perfect place to walk – the intimate scale makes driving difficult. The pink **La Valencia Hotel**, a popular retreat for the Hollywood set, is the landmark building in town.

The Salk Institute
Spectacularly located high on the edge of a canyon overlooking the Pacific, the Salk Institute was established by polio vaccine discoverer Jonas Salk as an environment that would stimulate original thinking. The surreal concrete building that houses the Institute was designed by Louis Kahn in 1960.
10010 North Torre Pines Rd, San Diego. Tours can be arranged in advance by calling (858) 453 4100, ext 200. www.salk.edu

Birch Aquarium at Scripps
The best beaches in town stretch north of La Jolla up to the Scripps Institution of Oceanography, which is part of the University of California.

The aquarium here displays the marine life of the Pacific, both in tanks and in an onshore tidepool, together with displays of the latest advances in oceanography.
8602 La Jolla Shores Drive, San Diego. Tel: (858) 534 3474. www.aquarium.ucsd.edu

University of California, San Diego
The beautiful UCSD campus just to the north of the Scripps Aquarium has an internationally acclaimed collection of commissioned site-specific sculpture.

Walking tours are given and brochures are available at the UCSD information kiosks at the Gilman Drive and North Torre Pines Road entrances.
Tel: (858) 534 3120. www.ucsd.edu

Maritime Museum of San Diego

This rather grandiose name is given to three ships moored on the Embarcadero.

The *Star of India*, built in 1863, is the oldest iron-hulled ship in America that is still afloat. Also here is the San Francisco Bay ferry-boat, *Berkeley*, which played a major role in evacuating victims of the 1906 earthquake, and a 1904 steam yacht, the *Medea*, which still makes occasional trips around San Diego Bay.

1306 North Harbor Drive, San Diego.
Tel: (619) 234 9153.
www.sdmaritime.com.
Open: daily 9am–8pm.
Admission charge.

Mission Bay Park

If it can be done on water, it can be done in Mission Bay. This city-owned aquatic park is the biggest of its kind in the world.

Each watersport has its own designated area. There are six public swimming areas, which are off limits to boats. Water-skiers have their own 2.5km (1¹/₂-mile) straight course, and jet-skiers also have their own special area free from boat traffic.

At most of the bay's marinas you can buy, rent or charter almost anything that floats, from a kayak to a skiing speedboat. Sailing and windsurfing lessons are also available at reasonable rates.

Landlubbers can rent bicycles for leisurely rides along the many bike trails over the 1,862 hectares (4,600 acres), and there are over 32km (20 miles) of running paths for joggers and walkers.

For the less active there are plenty of fish to be caught, and tackle can be rented by the day.

For the non-active there is not much sightseeing. The landscape is flat and is not significantly different from watersports areas in other places. There is, however, one attraction that never fails to impress visitors of any age.

Sea World

This is the marine equivalent of Disneyland, a fantasy land inhabited by all forms of marine life. This 55-hectare (135-acre) park features six major shows that are alternately staged throughout the day at stadiums and indoor auditoriums. Between shows, one can touch or view live animals at 20 educational exhibits and four aquariums.

Sea World really deserves a whole day to do it justice, but if time is limited there are two shows that must not be missed.

The number-one attraction is without doubt Baby Shamu, a young killer whale born in the park. The **Shamu Show** in the Shamu Stadium is a must. The other not-to-be-missed production is **Pirates of Pinniped** starring a talented troupe of sea lions, otters and a spitting walrus.

Of the exhibits, the **Dolphin Pool** is always very popular and a true

encounter experience. The dolphins love to be petted by the visitors. Similarly, the **Penguin Encounter**, where you can watch the largest penguin colony north of the Antarctic, never fails to please.

For a different perspective of the park take either the Southwest Skytower or the Skyride to give you a bird's-eye view of both Sea World and the whole of Mission Bay.
1720 South Shores Rd, San Diego. Tel: (619) 226 3901; www.seaworld.com. Admission charge.

Star of India, Maritime Museum of San Diego

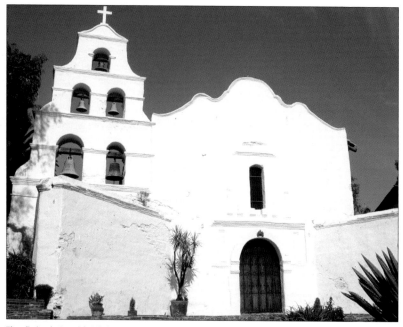

The distinctly Spanish Mission San Diego de Alcala, San Diego

Mission Valley

Considering the historic importance of Father Junípero Serra's first mission in California, **Mission San Diego de Alcala** is in a curiously suburban setting. The mission is really the only site of interest in the valley and is refreshingly uncommercial.

The original mission was built in 1769 but was moved a few years later because of disputes between the Spanish and the Indians. The second mission was burned down by the Indians in 1775 and the present mission was constructed in 1777. Destroyed by an earthquake in 1803, all that remains now is a church with a bell tower and a small museum set in beautiful gardens.

10818 San Diego Mission Rd, San Diego. Tel: (619) 281 8449. www.missionsandiego.com. Open: daily 9am–5pm. Admission charge.

Old Town

Old Town is where San Diego began; it was the first European settlement in California.

The State of California bought six blocks of historic buildings in the 1960s and established the **Old Town State Historic Park** in 1967. The core of the park is a traditional Mexican plaza around which many of the old buildings are located. Altogether there are 16 historic structures, of which 10 house museums – there are also 33 craft and speciality shops and seven restaurants! This commercial element tends to be concentrated on the **Bazaar del Mundo**, a loud and garish shopping and restaurant complex immediately off the main plaza. Fortunately most of the visitors tend to congregate here, leaving the rest of the park relatively quiet, and thus preserving the historic atmosphere of the area.

A self-guided walking tour brochure is available free of charge at the Visitor Center in the **Robinson Rose House**, or free guided tours are available every day at 2pm outside the Visitor Center.
Old Town San Diego State Historic Park, 4002 Wallace St, San Diego.
Tel: (858) 220 5422.
www.parks.ca.gov/?page_id=663.
Museums open: weekends 10am–5pm.

Point Loma
A drive out to the **Cabrillo National Monument** at Point Loma is worth it if only for the view. On a clear day there is a sweeping view from La Jolla all the way to Mexico.

During the winter this is the ideal place to watch hundreds of California grey whales on their annual migration from Alaska to their breeding grounds off the coast of Baja California in Mexico.

The museum here is only of passing interest and in itself would barely justify the 16km (10-mile) drive out from San Diego. The nearby statue of Cabrillo is equally unimpressive.

The restored **Old Point Loma Lighthouse** is a short walk away and open for visits. For hikers, there are plenty of trails down to the shore of the peninsula.

To reach Point Loma from San Diego take Rosencrans Street to Catalina Boulevard and then follow Cabrillo Memorial Drive until you arrive at the monument.

Seaport Village
This modern shopping and dining complex, only a few minutes' walk from the very heart of downtown San Diego, is intended to depict the harbourside as it was a century ago. It is difficult to believe that it could have been so well manicured back then, but it does provide a very agreeable environment for shopping, with pleasant landscaped walks overlooking the harbour.

Some 6 hectares (14 acres) have been developed with over 60 shops and 17 restaurants, and there are ambitious extension works planned.

Living history: soldier re-enactor in front of Robinson-Rose House, Old Town Visitor Center, San Diego

California parks

California is blessed with the most diverse scenic national parks in the USA. Towering coastal redwoods in the north, bubbling mud at volcanic Mount Lassen, giant rock faces at Yosemite, sand dunes of Death Valley – it would be difficult to imagine a more spectacular collection of natural wonders.

The great Scottish naturalist, John Muir, actively lobbied for the protection of the great mountain wilderness areas of the Sierra Nevada, and, in 1890, Sequoia was the second National Park to be created after Yellowstone in Wyoming, and Yosemite was created just a few weeks later. The most recent National Park creations were Death Valley and Joshua Tree in the 1990s.

If that is not enough, 526,091 hectares (1.3 million acres) of California has been dedicated to over 270 State Parks. Many of these State Parks are the equal of their Big Brother National Parks both in size and variety. Anza Borrego, on the Mexican border, covers 242,811 hectares (600,000 acres) and several different ecosystems, while Fort Ross on the Northern Sonoma Coast covers just a few hectares preserving a handful of early 19th-century buildings from Russia's farthest outpost. California's State Parks make up the most diverse natural and cultural park system in the nation.

Whether it's lighthouses, vestiges of colonial Russia, Spanish-era adobe buildings or rhododendron reserves, there is something to interest almost everyone. California is the birthplace of mountain biking, and 4,828km (3,000 miles) of hiking, biking and equestrian trails provide endless opportunities for adventure. Combine this with 1,006km (625 miles) of lake and river frontage, 451km (280 miles) of coast and 18,000 campsites and you can spend months here without leaving the State Park system.

Facing page: Joshua trees at sunset, Mojave National Preserve
Above: El Capitan in winter, Yosemite National Park; below: Artist's Drive, Death Valley National Park

The deserts

No visitor to California should leave without at least one visit to the desert. In the southern part of the state the desert is all around you and within a couple of hours' drive from almost anywhere you can be in the middle of an arid wilderness. Much of the desert is a flat, barren, dusty landscape with little to commend it to the visitor. However, there are large areas of great beauty and interest that have been designated as national or state parks.

The best time to visit the deserts is between late autumn and mid-May when temperatures are at their most comfortable level. Summer can be sizzling, but because the air is so dry it is rarely totally unbearable and the evenings are always cool and sometimes cold. Remember it is always a good idea to take water with you, even when driving on main roads, in case of a breakdown. You may well need it in the heat, and in many places traffic is infrequent at best.

Anza-Borrego
This is one of the largest state parks in continental US. Over 2,590 sq km (1,000 square miles) of badlands and mountains extend from the Colorado Desert to the great Sonoran Desert across the border in Mexico.

The desert was first crossed by Spanish explorer Juan Bautista de Anza in 1774 and he was commemorated by having his name added to Borrego, Spanish for the bighorn sheep now only found in the more remote corners of the park.

This is not a place for fast sightseeing. There are over 965km (600 miles) of roads, mostly unmetalled, and as many footpaths. The best way to experience Anza-Borrego is to explore on foot. Nature walks are led by rangers from the visitor centre during weekends and holidays in season.

The variety of desert plants is the highlight of the park and there are several walks that show a

DESERT WILDLIFE

To the casual visitor the desert regions may appear barren and empty but as many as 75 species of mammal make their home here. Two-thirds of these are rodents which have most successfully adapted to the desert habitat. Larger mammals include the kit fox, the coyote and bighorn sheep.

The temperature extremes experienced in the desert regions have forced most mammals to become nocturnal, and the best chance of sighting an animal is at dawn or dusk or in the light of car headlamps.

Reptiles are more commonly seen. Several kinds of lizard are found throughout the region, along with five kinds of rattlesnake and the sidewinder (although snakes are by no means a common sight).

In spring the deserts are alive with birds – the cheeky roadrunner, of all desert wildlife, symbolises nature's ability to conquer hostile environments.

good cross-section in a short distance.
Particularly notable are the California
fan palms, ocotillos, smoke trees and the
elephant tree which is unique to Anza-
Borrego in North America.

If you have the energy to climb some
of the steeper trails, you will be
rewarded with magnificent displays of
several varieties of cactus.

For a good view of the badlands drive
up to Font's Point north of Borrego
Palm Canyon.

By car, Anza-Borrego is one-and-a-
half hours south of Palm Springs and
two hours east of San Diego.

Anza-Borrego Visitor Center

Three miles west of Borrego Springs,
at Borrego Palm Canyon, the visitor
centre and museum sit buried in the
desert. The building is partially
underground, covered with cement and
six feet of sand. Outside the museum is
a comprehensive cactus garden.

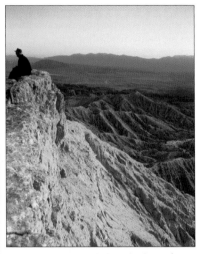

Anza-Borrego State Park desert landscape from
Font's Point at sunset

*Anza-Borrego State Park, PO Box 299,
Borrego Springs, California 92004.
Tel: (760) 767 5311.
www.parks.ca.gov/?page_id=668*

Anza-Borrego State Park Visitor Center

Death Valley

In spite of its forbidding name, very few people have actually died here.

It was Christmas Day 1849 when the first white man gazed down at Death Valley. What has become known as the Death Valley Party consisted of four families and a group of young men. They were on their way from Salt Lake City looking for an easy way across the Sierra Nevada to the newly discovered gold fields in the San Joaquin Valley.

Twenty-six wagons went into Death Valley but only one made it out. One person died and it is said that the valley was given its name when one of the party looked back as they were leaving and said, 'Goodbye, death valley'.

Today Death Valley is a national park with over 805km (500 miles) of well-maintained roads and nearly all the attractions only a short walk away.

Death Valley is unique among desert valleys, not only because of its size and variety of scenery, but also because of its extremes.

It has the lowest point in the western hemisphere at 86m (282ft) below sea level, but Telescope Peak rises to over 3,353m (11,000ft) not far away. Only 97km (60 miles) to the west is Mount Whitney, at 4,418m (14,495ft), the highest peak in continental US outside Alaska.

In 1913 a record high air temperature of 57°C (134°F) was recorded and summer temperatures regularly exceed 49°C (120°F), making it undoubtedly one of the hottest places on earth.

Badwater, Death Valley, where a ground temperature of 74°C (165°F) has been recorded

Artist's Drive

Just south of Furnace Creek on Highway 178 a dirt road branches off into the Black Mountains. **Artist's Drive**, as it is called, makes a nine-mile loop through some of the most barren but colourful landscape in the world. Minerals have leached out of the ground and created a breathtaking display of colour splashed across the mountainsides.

Although Artist's Drive is not paved it is well maintained and accessible to two-wheel-drive vehicles.

Badwater

The lowest point in the western hemisphere is only a short walk down from Highway 178. A pond of saline water permanently occupies this depression even in the hottest months, and in the early morning you can see the reflection of Telescope Peak to the west.

There are extensive salt flats just beyond Badwater. Walking out on to them is like entering a crystalline world of dazzling white stretching for as far as the eye can see.

Borax Museum

In Furnace Creek there is an outdoor museum dedicated to the mineral that made fortunes in Death Valley. There is a collection of old stagecoaches, wagons and mining equipment. The oldest house in Death Valley is here, built in 1883.

Two miles north is the Harmony Borax Works, the ruins of the valley's first borax plant. An original 20-mule-team rig, looking as sturdy as it must have done in 1907, stands in front of the ruin.

Dante's View

Twenty-seven miles from Furnace Creek and 1,670m (5,478ft) high, Dante's View gives a 360-degree bird's-eye panorama of Death Valley National Monument. Badwater lies one vertical mile below as you gaze out across the desolate landscape.

If you are up here in the early morning or late evening, take along a sweater. The temperature can be 10°C (20°F) cooler than in the valley. Also, look out for tarantulas. In the autumn these big, hairy but generally harmless spiders are out in their hundreds looking for mates, and you can usually see them crossing the road up to Dante's View.

Devil's Golf Course

A dirt road off Highway 190 between Stovepipe Wells and Furnace Creek takes you to strange salt towers and brine pools. The salt here is up to 1.5m (5ft) thick and almost as pure as table salt.

Furnace Creek

Nearby springs have enabled Furnace Creek to become not only the geo-graphical but also the commercial centre of Death Valley. Not that there is much here. Two hotels, two campsites, a couple of restaurants and shops and a very large caravan site which in the winter is full of retired people escaping to the sun.

There is also the Death Valley National Park Visitor Center which has a small museum and information centre. During the summer this air-conditioned retreat can be a very welcome relief. *Tel: (760) 786 3200. www.nps.gov/deva. Open: daily 8am–5pm throughout the year (until 9pm Nov–Apr).*

Scotty's Castle

By far the single biggest visitor attraction in Death Valley is both man-made and totally incongruous.

At the far northern end of the valley, just off Highway 267 close to Ubehebe Crater, a flamboyant rogue and sometime prospector, nicknamed Death Valley Scotty, persuaded Chicago millionaire Albert Johnson to build an extravagant Spanish-style mansion in the desert. Scotty had originally lured Johnson out here with bogus tales of a gold mine. Johnson, however, found that the climate suited his fragile health, forgave Scotty and the two became lifelong friends.

The 25-room house has a 15m (50ft) high living room, a music room with a 1,600-pipe organ, and even indoor waterfalls that acted as air-conditioners in the summer.

The house is now administered by the National Park Service.
Death Valley National Park,
CA 92328. Tel: (760) 786 2331.
Admission charge.

Stovepipe Wells

Although this is the valley's only other town after Furnace Creek it consists of nothing more than a store, motel, restaurant and petrol station.

However, six miles down the road is a remarkable area of sand dunes. Dawn is the best time to walk into them when the footprints of the previous day's visitors have been blown away and the low dawn light casts long shadows over the sand.

Ubehebe Crater

At the northern end of the park a volcanic explosion created this huge crater 1km (^{1}/$_2$ mile) across and 122m (400ft) deep. A short walk from the car park takes you to the high point on the crater rim, with dramatic views of Death Valley against the Black Mountains.

Zabriskie Point

Take Highway 190 for 6km (4 miles) east of Furnace Creek and turn off to the Zabriskie Point lookout for one of the best panoramic views of the southern half of Death Valley.

Early morning and late afternoon light is particularly beautiful, and if you have time the best walk in the valley goes from Zabriskie Point down through the badlands, across the foot of Manly Beacon and on through Golden Canyon.

A low-rise façade hides baronial splendour within Scotty's Castle

The 4km (2¹/₂-mile) trail walk takes under two hours, but you need to arrange for a lift back up to the lookout car park.

Joshua Tree National Park

The high Mojave Desert meets the low Colorado Desert here at Joshua Tree. The park was named after the thousands of spiky, tree-like plants that are actually giant members of the lily family. These 'trees' grow only at altitudes between 914m and 1,524m (3,000–5,000ft) and can reach heights of 12m (40ft).

The most impressive groups of plants are in the high western part of the park. The road passes by enormous, rounded granite boulders that are scattered through the landscape. These provide a platform for gymnastic displays by rock climbers.

There are three entrances to the park, from Highway 62 at Joshua Tree or Twentynine Palms, and in the south, via Cottonwood Springs Road off I-10.

Oasis Visitor Center

The best way to enter the park is from the town of Twentynine Palms. The Visitor Center will supply maps and trail guides as well as brochures and general information. There is also a shop and small museum at this entrance.

Cholla Cactus Garden

Winding down from the Mojave into the Colorado Desert the landscape changes from rugged rocks and mountains into a barren, flat expanse of parched earth.

The Cholla Cactus Garden is a forest of Opuntia cacti that manages to survive in this harsh environment. One of the

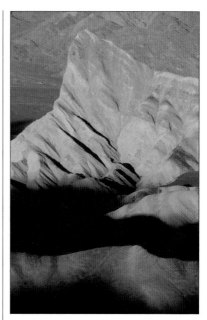

Zabriskie Point at dawn, Death Valley National Park

prettiest walks in the park passes through here, but be warned: the other name for the cholla is 'jumping cactus' and with good reason; although they do not actually jump, the plants have an annoying tendency to attach themselves to you with even the slightest touch. They rarely grow higher than 1m (3ft), but the length of their spines makes up for their lack of height! Also keep an eye open for the five types of rattlesnake that live here, if you want to avoid a potentially nasty encounter. *Joshua Tree National Park, 74485 National Park Drive, Twentynine Palms, CA 92277. Tel: (760) 367 5500. www.nps.gov/jotr. Visitor centres open daily 8am–4pm. Admission charge.*

Palm Springs

To anyone in southern California 'the desert' means Palm Springs and its equally affluent neighbours, Rancho Mirage and Palm Desert.

Before the 1920s this was a sleepy little health spa where people came for the hot springs and dry air. Then it was discovered by Hollywood.

Palm Springs rapidly grew to become one of the world's major winter resorts. The skies are always blue, the air always clear, and the golf courses, all 84 of them, always green.

There is even cross-country skiing up on Mount San Jacinto, towering 2,621m (8,600ft) above Palm Springs.

'The Season' for 'the desert' starts in January and continues through to the end of April. To be seen here before Christmas or after Easter is just not done, unless, of course, you want the best rates at hotels and some great travel bargains. The summer can be very hot, but the discounts available can almost make the temperatures bearable. However, many attractions close or have limited hours during the summer. Always telephone in advance.

Moorten's Botanical Garden

This 1.6-hectare (4-acre) garden displays over 3,000 different varieties of cactus and other desert plants. You will also see plenty of lizards, birds and dinosaur fossils throughout the garden.
1701 S Palm Canyon Drive, Palm Springs. Tel: (760) 327 6555. Open: daily 9am–4.30pm. Admission charge.

Palm Springs Aerial Tramway

A cable-car ride to the summit of

Mount San Jacinto is one of Palm Springs' most popular attractions. This mile-high ride provides views from Joshua Tree across to the Salton Sea with the whole of the Palm Springs valley in the foreground.

At the top of the mountain, apart from the usual restaurant, bar and souvenir shops, there is a short nature trail, and mules are available for 20-minute rides around the slopes.

Depending upon snow conditions, usually from late November to mid-April, the **Nordic Ski Center** is open for cross-country ski excursions.
Aerial Tramway tel: (760) 325 1391. www.pstramway.com. Open: Mon–Fri 10am–8pm, weekends & holidays 8am–8pm. Admission charge. San Jacinto Ranger Station: Tel: (760) 327 0222. Nordic Ski Center: Tel: (760) 325 3490.

Palm Springs Desert Museum

This museum has an eclectic assortment of exhibits from western American art to desert natural history to Indian basketry. It is a collection of considerable regional importance and worth a visit if only for the delightfully landscaped sculpture garden.
101 Museum Drive, Palm Springs. Tel: (760) 325 0189. www.psmuseum.org. Open: Sept–early June, Tue–Fri 10am–4pm, weekends 10am–5pm. Admission charge.

Village Green Heritage Center

In the middle of the exclusive shops and restaurants of **Palm Canyon Drive**, three old buildings from Palm Springs' past look almost too perfect to be genuine.

The **McCallum Adobe** was built in 1884 and is the town's oldest building. Next door is Cornelia White's 1893 home made from railroad ties, and then there is **Ruddy's General Store**. The store is a re-creation of a typical 1930s general store complete with shelves stocked with over 6,000 genuine items from the period. It is one of the most complete displays of unused general store merchandise in the country.

221 South Palm Canyon Drive, Palm Springs. Tel: (760) 323 8297. www.palmsprings.com/history. Open: Oct–June, Thur–Sun 10am–4pm; July–Sept, weekends only 10am–4pm. Admission charge.

Palm Desert

This rival of Palm Springs is rapidly becoming one of the desert's major resort towns. The quality of shops along **El Paseo** is exceptional, equal to that of Rodeo Drive in Los Angeles. The town obviously caters to visitors who do not have to worry too much about money.

Apart from shopping, **The Living Desert** is the other attraction that should not be missed in Palm Desert.

This 486-hectare (1,200-acre) garden and wild animal park re-creates eight different desert habitats. There is even a display of nocturnal animals in a special enclosure.

47900 South Portola Ave, Palm Desert. Tel: (619) 346 5694. Open: Sept–mid-June, daily 9am–5pm. Admission charge.

Rancho Mirage

The only reason to visit Rancho Mirage is to see how the other half lives. This extremely wealthy bedroom community between Palm Springs and Palm Desert was home to Bob Hope and Frank Sinatra – both have streets named after them.

There is little of interest for the visitor.

Salton Sea

This vast body of water was formed in 1905 when the Colorado River poured billions of gallons of flood water into this desert area that lies below sea level. There are no natural outlets and over the years evaporation has concentrated the salinity of the water.

It is a major link in the Pacific Flyway, and thousands of birds use the sea either as a stopover or to spend the winter. One-third of all North America's white pelican population winter here.

Nearby Coachella Valley is the centre of the California date growers, and the roads are lined with alternating date-palm groves and shops selling gift-wrapped dates.

Lush Indian canyons in Palm Springs

Highway One
The coastal route

From Santa Monica to San Francisco, California Highway 1 hugs the coast all the way and en route passes through some of the finest scenery and most interesting towns in the state. This is certainly the very best way to travel from Los Angeles to San Francisco, and it ranks as one of the finest drives in the nation, sandwiched as it is between mountains and sea.

A section of the Big Sur coast

Los Angeles is the best place to start. The drive gets increasingly interesting and spectacular as you drive north. At least two days should be allocated for this trip, which will allow you time for some brief sightseeing stops. The entries from pages 68 to 71 and pages 74 to 75 are arranged in the order in which you would meet them on the road.

Santa Barbara

Santa Barbara is one of the most beautiful towns in the country. It sits on a curving, sandy bay with the Santa Ynez Mountains as a backdrop. Add to this a near-perfect climate and you have the closest an American town gets to paradise.

The Spanish named it *la tierra adorada* – the beloved land. A massive earthquake destroyed the town in 1925 and left the way clear to plan a whole new town based on its Spanish roots. Present-day Santa Barbara is mainly Spanish and mission-style architecture with red tile roofs and a strong Mediterranean flavour. Whitewashed walls and elegant palm trees complete the effect.

It seems, however, that there is always trouble in paradise. In 1989 a devastating fire swept through the hills of Santa Barbara, and there is a continuing water shortage of mammoth proportions.

Nevertheless, none of this has prevented an increasing number of Hollywood stars from settling here.

The first stop in Santa Barbara should be the Visitor Information Center at 1 Santa Barbara Street (*tel: (805) 965 3021. www.santabarbara.com/community/ visitors_center*).

Ask for maps of the 'Red Tile Tour' for walkers and the 'Scenic Drive'. The street layout can be confusing and a detailed map of the town is invaluable.

County Courthouse

This Spanish-Moorish castle was built in 1929 and remains the grandest building in town. A visit to the top of the bell tower gives an unparalleled view of Santa Barbara and the bay. *1100 Anacapa St. Tel: (805) 962 6464.*

www.santabarbara.com/points_of_interest /courthouse. *Open: daily 9am–5pm. Free admission.*

El Presidio de Santa Barbara State Historic Park

The site is still being excavated and restored and there are two buildings, El Cuartel and La Cañedo Adobe, that were part of the original Spanish fort blessed by Father Junípero Serra in 1782. A reconstructed chapel and padre's quarters complete the site. *129 East Cañon Perdido St. Tel: (805) 965 0093. www.sbthp.org/presidio. Open: Mon–Fri 10.30am–4.30pm, Sat & Sun noon–4pm. Free admission.*

Mission Santa Barbara

This is the grandest of the missions established by the Spanish and is often called 'The Queen of Missions'. Founded in 1786, it sits on a knoll high above the town and its design was based on the designs of Roman engineers dating back to AD 27.

There is a small museum, and the gardens are particularly worth seeing. *2201 Laguna St. Tel: (805) 682 4149. www.sbmission.org. Open: weekdays 9am–5pm, Sun 1–5pm. Admission charge.*

Stearns Wharf

This is the oldest pier on the West Coast and is an extension of Santa Barbara's main street, State Street. It was built in 1872 and has the usual mixture of souvenir shops, cafés, restaurants and seafood stands.

At the end of the pier you can probably see the once-endangered brown pelicans trying to sneak fish from the anglers, who seem to be a permanent fixture here.

San Luis Obispo

The fifth mission built by Junípero Serra is located here, but its ruins are not of any particular interest.

San Luis Obispo is a college town focused around the California Polytechnic State University, which has one of the finest agricultural faculties in the country.

Though the town does not offer a great deal that is of interest to visitors, it does provide a pleasant break on the drive up Highway 1.

Santa Barbara County Courthouse

San Simeon

Forty miles north of San Luis Obispo, newspaper magnate William Randolph Hearst built what must be the most opulent and extravagant 'house' in California if not the nation.

Starting in 1919, **Hearst Castle** took 30 years to build at a cost of three million dollars. Today it is estimated that the building would cost 300 to 400 million dollars to complete.

There are 38 bedrooms, 14 sitting rooms, two libraries, a kitchen and a theatre, and all this is just in the main house. There are two additional buildings that are guesthouses.

The property is so big that four different tours are offered by the State Park Service, which has administered the property since 1957.

It is the second-biggest attraction in California, after Disneyland, with over a million visitors a year. Because of its popularity reservations are essential at the height of the season and are recommended at all times.

Each tour takes two hours, and for the first-time visitor Tour 1 is the best introduction. Wear comfortable shoes, there is a lot of walking to do!
To make reservations call toll-free (800) 444 4445 within California or (916) 414 8400/4100 out of state.
www.hearstcastle.com. Open: daily, except for New Year's Day, Thanksgiving & Christmas. Admission charge.

Big Sur

Big Sur is specifically the name of a small town about 32km (20 miles) south of Carmel, but it has come to be synonymous with a section of dramatic coastline that extends from the Carmel Highlands down to San Simeon.

The 145km (90-mile) drive clings precariously to the side of the Santa Lucia Mountains. It is a tortuous two-lane road that takes several hours to drive, but the dramatic scenery more than justifies the journey.

Lookout points are provided all along the route and during the winter months give a bird's-eye view of the California grey whales on their annual migration to and from Mexico. The road passes four state parks and hundreds of square kilometres of wilderness, spread east of Highway 1, and it is penetrated by numerous hiking trails.

For many years this was a favourite hideaway for literary giants such as Henry Miller and Hollywood stars Rita Hayworth and Orson Welles.
For information on accommodation and attractions contact: Big Sur Chamber of Commerce, Box 87, Big Sur, California 93920. Tel: (831) 667 2100.
www.bigsurcalifornia.org

Point Lobos State Reserve

Robert Louis Stevenson wrote that Point Lobos was 'the most beautiful meeting of land and sea on earth'.

The Pacific Ocean constantly pounds the granite coast to create a bizarre and beautiful landscape capped by Monterey pines.

This 506-hectare (1,250-acre) state park just south of Carmel is easily accessible by road, but the parking areas are small so in summer it pays to get there early.

Several trails exist in the park, but for a short visit the Cypress Grove Trail should not be missed and will give a good introduction to this part of the coastline. Look out for the playful sea otters that frolic in the kelp forests off Point Lobos.

Trail maps and wildlife guides are available from the ranger station at the park entrance.
Tel: (831) 624 4909. www.pt-lobos.parks.state.ca.us. Open: daily 9am–4pm (until sunset in summer).

Carmel

This small village by the sea is one of northern California's biggest tourist attractions.

Originally Carmel was a haven for artists and writers, but they have long since been priced out of the market. The art galleries remain, however – all 70 of them! It is a town that is almost too perfect. There are no neon signs, no traffic lights, no hoardings or bill-boards. There is no postal delivery so all 5,000 residents have to collect their mail from the post office. There are no house numbers or parking meters. There are even laws against eating in the street and wearing high heels. Needless to say, fast-food restaurants are not allowed.

This forced effort to remain 'quaint' attracts so many people during the summer, especially at weekends, that it is almost impossible to move. Parking in particular becomes extremely difficult.

There is no denying that Carmel does have considerable charm, but try to avoid weekends. It is a place to visit for ambience rather than sightseeing. The beach is particularly fine (*see p72*), and so is the mission.

Mission San Carlos Borromeo del Carmelo

The Carmel Mission was the favourite of Father Junípero Serra, who lies buried in the church. It was the second mission in the chain, built in 1771, and it remained Serra's headquarters until his death. It is located on a splendid site at the mouth of the Carmel River, overlooking the sea.

Extensive restoration has returned the mission to its original condition, and it is perhaps the most authentic and beautiful mission in the chain.
3080 Rio Rd, Carmel. Tel: (831) 624 1271. www.carmelmission.org. Open: Mon–Sat 9.30am–4.30pm, Sun 10.30am–4.30pm.

The exclusive residential and golfing community of Pebble Beach adjoins Carmel and can be reached from Ocean Ave (see p76).

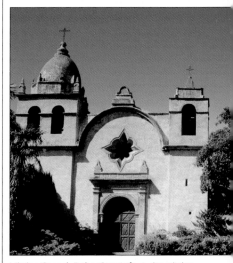

Mission Carmel, Father Serra's favourite mission

Walk: Carmel

Carmel is the jewel of the central California coast, and this walk through the town and along the beach will show the best that Carmel has to offer. It is located only 2 hours south of San Francisco.

Allow 2 hours.

The best place to start is at the junction of Dolores St and Ocean Ave. The popularity of Carmel combined with the limited amount of parking available is a perennial problem. There is a small public car park at the end of Ocean Ave, but apart from that there are only 2-hour parking meters. Fortunately the town is so small that nowhere is too far.

1 Ocean Avenue

This is the main shopping street in Carmel with an enticing collection of boutiques and art galleries. Off Ocean Avenue is a rabbit warren of alleyways and courtyards crammed with even more shops, galleries and restaurants.

Carmel has long been associated with the arts, particularly photography. Just off Ocean Avenue at 6th and Dolores, the Weston Gallery exhibits prints by Ansel Adams and Edward Weston among many other notable photographers. Photography West at Dolores and Ocean has a similarly impressive display of fine photographs. *Walk down Ocean Ave towards the ocean. At the car parking area walk on to the beach and turn left.*

2 The beach

The best way to experience this walk to the full is to throw off your shoes and socks and get the sand between your toes. Even in December and January the weather can be sunny and warm, and this is one of the best stretches of sand on the coast. The beach sweeps around to the rocks at the southern tip of Carmel Bay.

You do not have to walk on the sand. Scenic Road runs parallel to the beach and it was not named accidentally. It gives unequalled views of the coast.

However, it is better to start on the beach as the first section of Scenic Road does not have a footpath and cars can come perilously close on this narrow street. Scenic Road can be reached from the beach at several points by easily spotted wooden steps.

The sandy beach ends at a group of surf-spattered rocks at the southern end. It is possible to scramble over these rocks but it is far safer to climb up the last wooden steps to the footpath by Scenic Road if you have not already done so.

Continue south on the footpath.

3 Tor House

After a short distance you will see a house jutting out spectacularly over the sea. Look left and there you will see a medieval-looking stone tower and a rambling house constructed from huge boulders. This was the home of the great American poet, Robinson Jeffers.

To get to the house turn left up Stewart Way and then left again on to Ocean View Avenue. Tor House is two houses down on the left.

Jeffers built the house and tower with his own hands, hauling the granite stones by horse from the little cove below. The house was modelled after an English Tudor barn, and took him less than four years to complete. Jeffers built it using a block and tackle system and wooden planks, similar to methods used by the ancient Egyptians. He lived here from 1919 until his death in 1962. One wing of the house is still occupied by his daughter-in-law, Lee. Hawk Tower was built as a retreat for his wife.

Tor House is open for tours on Fridays and Saturdays between 10am and 4pm, strictly by appointment. For reservations *tel: (831) 624 1813* or write to The Tor House Foundation, Box 1887, Carmel, California 93921.

Return to Ocean Ave by the same route.

A walker's view of Tor House, Carmel

Mural depicting the traditional fishing industry on Cannery Row, Monterey

Monterey

In the early years of California, Monterey was the most important city. It was the Spanish capital of Alta California, then the Mexican capital in 1822, and the American capital in 1846.

After the discovery of gold the focus of the state moved north and Monterey became a major fishing port. Today it is tourism that keeps its economy afloat.

Cannery Row

This street of old fish canneries filled with eccentric characters was immortalised by John Steinbeck. Gentrification has destroyed the old atmosphere and it is now just another tourist trap.

The aquarium at the far end of the wharf is the one notable exception. (*See also below.*)

Fisherman's Wharf

The wharf was built in 1846 as a pier for trading ships coming around Cape Horn. It was also used by sardine fishermen and whaling boats before the fishing industry hit the doldrums.

It has now gone the way of Cannery Row and is little more than a tourists' shopping and restaurant mall. There are, however, good views of the bay from the end of the wharf.

Monterey Bay Aquarium

The importance of this aquarium extends far beyond the Monterey

JOHN STEINBECK

Most of Steinbeck's writings were based on Monterey or Salinas, where he was born in 1902. To support himself through Stanford University, which he attended intermittently between 1919 and 1926, he worked as a labourer. His first novel to achieve popular success, *Tortilla Flat*, was based on real-life experiences with the agricultural workers of Monterey County.

The Grapes of Wrath was published in 1937, and in the same year appeared as both a stage play and a film. The book won a Pulitzer Prize and established Steinbeck as a major American writer.

Several books followed, including *Of Mice and Men*, *Cannery Row* and *East of Eden*, but none reached the critical success of his work in the 1930s. In spite of this, in 1962, he was the seventh American writer to receive the Nobel Prize for Literature.

After spending most of his life in California, he died in New York in 1968.

peninsula. It is one of the finest and largest aquariums in the world, with over 6,500 marine creatures on exhibition. (*See also p79.*)
886 Cannery Row, Monterey. Tel: (831) 648 4888. Open: daily 10am–6pm. Admission charge.

Monterey's Path of History

A dozen historic buildings are on the walking tour through the oldest parts of Monterey. Entrance tickets can be bought at any of the buildings, and the ticket gives admission to all of them.

The Custom House at 1 Custom House Plaza is the most logical place to start. Across the road from Fisherman's Wharf, this important building is the oldest government office on the whole Pacific coast, and it was here that the US flag was first raised in 1846.
Maps of the self-guiding tour are available with ticket purchase. For opening times call (831) 649 7118.

Municipal Wharf

A small fishing fleet still uses this last working wharf in Monterey. Every day you can see boats unloading a wide variety of fish including tuna, swordfish, shark, squid, cod and salmon.

This is an ideal place to capture something of the flavour of the old Monterey of Steinbeck's time.

Pacific Grove

See p78.

Stevenson House

In California, it seems that wherever Robert Louis Stevenson spent a night has become a museum.

To be fair, he spent four months here in 1879, and the house at 530 Houston Street has been fully restored with 19th-century furnishings.
For details of opening times call: (831) 649 7118.
www.mchsmuseum.com/stevensonhouse. Admission charge.

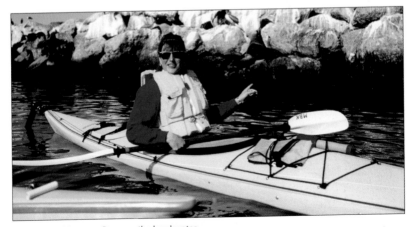

Kayaking on Monterey Bay near the breakwater

Tour: 17-Mile Drive, Pebble Beach

Pebble Beach is an exclusive residential development set amid forests and golf courses by a fabulously beautiful coastline. The 17-Mile Drive was originally named after the horse-drawn carriage ride from the Hotel Del Monte in Monterey out to the Del Monte Forest, though today it is much shorter than 17 miles (27km).

Allow 1½ hours

The drive can be started at either the southern entrance at the Carmel Gate on Ocean Avenue or in the north at the Pacific Grove Gate on Sunset Drive. It is virtually impossible to get lost as the whole drive is very well signposted.

Pebble Beach is a private estate and a toll is charged for using the road. This is refundable if you eat at the Pebble Beach Lodge.

Start at the Carmel Gate and turn right on to the 17-Mile Drive. Follow the signs.

1 Shepherd's Knoll

This high point on the drive gives spectacular views of Monterey Bay and the San Gablian Mountains.

The road passes through the Del Monte Forest and hillsides, covered with huckleberry bushes. Nestled in the woods are the luxurious homes of some of California's wealthiest families.

2 Spanish Bay and the Restless Sea

In 1769, Juan Gaspar de Portolá camped here while trying to locate Monterey Bay; today it is the perfect spot to have a picnic and watch the waves crash. Even on a calm day colliding ocean currents guarantee spectacular waves.

A walking trail along the coastal bluff starts here and continues past some of Monterey Bay's richest tidepools.

3 Seal and Bird Rocks

These landmark offshore rocks are home to a huge colony of shoreline birds, particularly the double-crested cormorant. There is also a large population of California sea lions and harbour seals that can be heard barking in the distance.

4 Spyglass Hill Golf Course

This is one of six golf courses at Pebble Beach and is rated in the top 40 in the USA. It is said that Robert Louis Stevenson was inspired by the view from this, his favourite hill, while writing *Treasure Island*. Each of the course's 18 holes takes its name from this classic.

As you drive by, it is not unusual to see deer sharing the golf courses with the golfers.

A view of shoreline and surf near Pebble Beach on the 17-Mile Drive

5 Cypress Point Lookout

The lookout gives one of the finest views of the coastline on 17-Mile Drive. On a clear day you can see as far as Point Sur Lighthouse, 32km (20 miles) south.

Immediately below the lookout is a breeding area for harbour seals, and in the spring the newborn seal pups can be watched from above.

6 The Lone Cypress

This solitary cypress clinging to an apparently bare rock has become one of California's most familiar landmarks. It is also the symbol of the Pebble Beach Company.

7 The Lodge at Pebble Beach

This famous resort, built in 1919, offers deluxe accommodation and restaurants with sweeping views of the ocean.

8 Pebble Beach Golf Course

This is considered by many to be the world's premier golf course. It opened at the same time as the Lodge in 1919 and has become the home of many of the great tournaments of North America.

Walk: Cannery Row and Pacific Grove

Cannery Row was immortalised by John Steinbeck's book of the same name. This walk combines superb coastal scenery with great marine wildlife viewing and passes through some of the most historic sections of Monterey.

Allow 2 hours, excluding a visit to the aquarium.

Start at the car park for Fisherman's Wharf off Del Monte Ave.

1 Fisherman's Wharf

This prime sightseeing attraction no longer attracts many fishermen. Commercial fishing is now based on the Municipal Wharf and the original Fisherman's Wharf is little more than a collection of souvenir shops and tourist restaurants. A couple of fish and crab stands still operate, but most of the wharf is a highly successful commercial venture and, judging by the crowds, apparently provides just what the tourist wants.

If you go all the way down to the end of the wharf you will be rewarded with excellent views of the harbour and the bay from the observation deck.

Turn right on to the footpath as soon as you leave Fisherman's Wharf and walk through Fisherman's Shoreline Park to the Coast Guard Wharf.

2 Coast Guard Wharf

In the winter months take the time to walk out to the end of the pier. Every year hundreds of California sea lions congregate here, and you can watch them basking in the sun from a few metres away.

Leaving the wharf, turn right on to Cannery Row, and follow it to the end.

3 Cannery Row

John Steinbeck knew and wrote about a very different Cannery Row to the one that now exists. Gone are the stinking fish canneries. They have been replaced by attractions such as the Steinbeck's Spirit of Monterey Wax Museum and the Paul Masson Winery Museum.

Only Doc Ricketts's Marine Lab at 800 Cannery Row stands relatively unchanged, although it is now a private club. And if you go down to the far end of Cannery Row you will come to Kalisa's La Ida Café, the only other remnant of the Steinbeck era.

The rest of the Row is now souvenir shops, restaurants and then more souvenir shops.

4 Monterey Bay Aquarium

This wonderful state-of-the-art aquarium is devoted exclusively to the marine life of Monterey Bay. At its heart and making up the centre-piece of the aquarium is a three-storey giant kelp forest that encapsulates life in the Bay.

There is also a 9m (30ft) deep sea otter tank, numerous tidepool and touching exhibits as well as outdoor observation decks.

From the aquarium follow the trail to Lover's Point in Pacific Grove. The trail overlooks the wild, rocky scenery of Monterey Bay.

5 Lover's Point

Pacific Grove is famous for the thousands of monarch butterflies that migrate through here every winter. The town is then transformed into 'Butterfly Town, USA'. A butterfly sculpture prominently displayed in the small park on this promontory sticking out into the bay serves as a year-long reminder of that event.

Take 17th St for two blocks and turn left on to Lighthouse Ave.

6 Lighthouse Avenue

Seventeenth Street enters Lighthouse Avenue in the middle of Pacific Grove's busy shopping area. A wide street lined with many interesting shops and some fine Victorian architecture, it has lots of charm.

Continue walking past a section of residential development to David Ave where Lighthouse Ave makes a sudden turn left and then right. You will find that the character of the avenue changes and the area gradually becomes much more cosmopolitan, with a wide range of ethnic restaurants and small shops.
Continue to the Presidio.

7 California's First Theatre

Pass through the Presidio and turn right on to Pacific Street, where you will find the first theatre built in California. It is still going strong with nightly performances of Victorian melodramas.

Cross Pacific St through the Custom House Mall and back to the Fisherman's Wharf car park.

Missions

In 1769, when Father Junípero Serra was already 55, he travelled 750 miles by donkey, from Mexico to San Diego, to build the first of a series of missions that would eventually extend up the coast of California as far as Sonoma to the north of San Francisco.

Junípero Serra had moved to Mexico from his birthplace in Majorca when he was 37. He was a small man with a pronounced limp, the result of an injury in Mexico for which he refused to have treatment. At the time of his death in 1784 he had travelled thousands of miles and established a further nine missions in what were then the remote outposts of California. He is buried in the second mission he founded at Carmel.

Serra was succeeded by Fermín Francisco de Lasuén who, like Serra, had moved to Mexico in his 30s. He established an additional eight missions during his 18 years in the office of president of the missions, and he was already 66 years old when he started the project. It was de Lasuén who developed the style of architecture that has come to be known throughout California as the mission style.

The missions were linked by El Camino Real – the King's Highway. Streets bearing the same name, following the original route, can be found in most of California's coastal towns today. Highway 101 closely follows this route.

All the missions are open to the public.

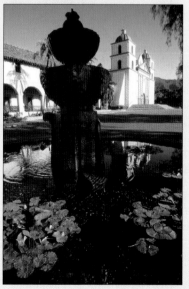

Facing page above: Santa Barbara, Queen of the Missions; below: Mission San Luis Rey de Francia
Above: interior, Mission Carmel church from the rear toward the altar; right: Santa Barbara Mission façade and fountain

San Francisco

San Francisco is everyone's favourite city. Its visual appeal has a lot to do with this. It is built on a series of hills that not only help to create an interesting architectural environment, but also allow glimpses of San Francisco Bay, the Golden Gate or the Pacific Ocean, as the city itself is surrounded on three sides by water.

Cable-car gripman and employees turning a cable car at the turnaround near Fisherman's Wharf

This spectacular location on a peninsula adds further to San Francisco's charm. The city is small. It covers only 119sq km (46 square miles) and has a population of less than 800,000. The scale is human, and it is one of the few North American cities that is both pleasant and manageable to walk around.

The climate helps its reputation too. It rarely gets too hot and almost never freezes. Natural air-conditioning keeps the air clean and sparkling for most of the time. It does, however, get cold, particularly in the summer when the famous sea fogs roll in from the Pacific. Just because it is August in California does not mean it is hot in San Francisco.

Within two years of James Marshall discovering gold in the Sierra Nevada, San Francisco grew from a population of 900 to 25,000. Forty years later it was over 300,000.

This cosmopolitan population, drawn by the lure of gold, set the pattern for the future. It is an international community with a great deal of tolerance. The city has the largest Oriental population outside the Orient, a Chinatown bigger than many towns in China and large Japanese, Vietnamese and Filipino communities. Then there

are the Mexicans. The Mission District is dominated by Spanish-speaking families from Mexico and Central America. You can spend a day there without hearing a word of English spoken. The Italians still have a very strong presence, although their traditional neighbourhood of North Beach is being invaded by Chinatown.

For well over a century San Francisco has retained its ethnic diversity, and its legendary tolerance has embraced the Beatniks of the 50s, the flower children of the 60s and now the largest gay population in the US.

Many of these factors have led to an active and progressive cultural scene. The opera and symphony orchestra are both of international standing. Both mainstream and experimental theatre are thriving. Many of the great 20th-century artists such as Mark Rothko and Clyfford Still have made their home here.

Most long-time residents rarely think of earthquakes, although the 1989 Loma Prieta shock jolted many people out of their complacency. All modern buildings have to be built to very rigorous standards and are considered to be virtually earthquake-proof. Even many of the older buildings have withstood severe shocks, including the 1906 disaster. Fire has always been a bigger danger than the actual quake.

In spite of the 1906 earthquake and several major fires, old San Francisco has remained remarkably well preserved. The old, painted Victorian houses have lost none of their charm even if they tend to be in some of the less desirable neighbourhoods. The cable cars still clank along as a living relic from the past, and Golden Gate Bridge commands the entrance to the bay as it has for the past 50 years.

People who have never visited California often speak of Los Angeles and San Francisco in the same breath, though in reality the two cities could not be more dissimilar, whether geographically, culturally or politically.

Cable cars

The first cable car ran in San Francisco in 1873, and at one time there were eight lines with over 177km (110 miles) of track. Today only three lines and 18km (11 miles) of track remain, but the cable car never loses its popularity.

The cable car does not have any form of power of its own. It moves by attaching a clamp to an endlessly moving cable below the tracks. To stop, the brakeman releases the clamp and applies the brakes. To move, he reattaches the clamp. At the end of the line the car must be turned around on a turntable and the passengers are often invited to lend some force to the task.

The quaint, clanking cars are as good a way to travel as any on San Francisco's congested streets, and the three operating lines cover several well-known tourist haunts. The Bay and Taylor cars leave Market Street, pass Chinatown and North Beach and finish at Fisherman's Wharf. Hyde and Beach cars also leave from Market Street, pass by Union Square, skirt around Chinatown, and travel on to Aquatic Park by Ghiradelli Square. The California Street line runs from the foot of California Street by the Hyatt Regency Hotel, up Nob Hill and on to Van Ness Avenue.

During the summer be prepared for long queues. It is best to buy tickets before boarding, and there are machines at the terminals and major stops.

To find out more about the history and workings of cable cars visit the **Cable Car Barn** on Mason Street. This is the main control centre, where you can see the actual cables running at precisely 15.3km/h ($9^1/_2$ mph) over 4m (14ft) pulleys called sheaves. There is also a good exhibit of old photographs, drawings and models, and some of the original cars built in 1873 by Andrew Hallidie.

Cable Car Barn, 1201 Mason St, San Francisco. Tel: (415) 474 1887. www.cablecarmuseum.org. Open: daily 10am–6pm. Free admission.

Tin How Temple in Chinatown, San Francisco

Alcatraz

Until its closure in 1963, The Rock, now administered by the National Parks Service, was home to some of America's most notorious criminals.

Most of the original cells, the hospital and dining room are open, and a self-guiding tour is available with a tape-recorded commentary by former inmates and guards. It takes about 1¹/₂ hours. There is also a special Alcatraz Night Tour, the proceeds of which go to support preservation and restoration projects on Alcatraz and throughout the Golden Gate National Parks.

This is one of the most popular attractions in San Francisco, so make your ferry bookings as far ahead as possible. Remember to take some warm clothing and wear comfortable shoes. *Ferries leave from Pier 41 next to Fisherman's Wharf starting at 9am, with the last boat leaving at 5pm in the summer and 3pm in the winter. The Night Tour operates all year Thur–Mon evenings. Tel: (415) 705 5555. www.nps.gov/alcatraz*

California Palace of the Legion of Honor

This neoclassical building was built in 1924 by the sugar millionaire Spreckels family, to honour the dead of World War I. The building was donated to the city and now houses a collection of European art. There is a fine collection of Rodin sculptures, including one of the original castings of *The Thinker*. *Lincoln Park, near 34th Ave & Clement St. Tel: (415) 863 3330. www.thinker.org. Open: Tue–Sun 9.30am–5pm. Admission charge.*

San Francisco

Alcatraz Island

Yerba
Buena
Island

Mexican Museum &
San Francisco   Maritime   Fisherman's   Pier 39
Craft & Folk Art Museum Museum   Wharf

N

Crissy Field
en Gate Promenade
MARINA BLVD

Marina
Green   Fort Mason   The Cannery

BAY ST

MARINA   Ghirardelli   North
Square   Beach

Coit
Tower

Palace of
Fine Arts

LOMBARD ST

COLUMBUS AVE

THE EMBARCADERO

Presidio
Army
Museum

Octagon House   Russian Hill

VAN NESS AVE

MASON ST

BROADWAY

Jackson
Square   Ferry Building

SIDIO

PACIFIC HEIGHTS

Haas-Lilienthal House

California Historical Society

Cable Car   Portsmouth
Barn   Square

HYDE ST

Nob Hill

MONTGOMERY ST

Transamerica Pyramid
Embarcadero
Center

80

Chinatown

WESTERN ADDITION

CALIFORNIA STREET

Grace Cathedral

101

n Francisco Fire Department
Pioneer Memorial Museum

POST ST

Japantown

Union Square

SAN FRANCISCO-
OAKLAND BAY
BRIDGE

gard BLVD

Duquette Foundation
Pavilion of St Francis   St Mary's
Cathedral

Moscone
Center

KEARNY STREET

University of
San Francisco

TURK STREET

DIVISADERO STREET

WESTERN
ADDITION

MASONIC AVE

Alamo
Square   FELL ST

Civic
Center

Old U.S. Mint

SOUTH
OF
MARKET

HOWARD STREET

FOLSOM STREET

VAN NESS AVE

3RD ST

4TH ST

Pacific Bell Park

China
Basin

de Young
eum

Panhandle

LOWER
HAIGHT

Buena
Vista Park

10TH ST

6TH ST

101

San
Francisco
Bay

nia Academy
Sciences

STANYAN STREET

PARNASSUS AVE

HAIGHT-
ASHBURY

14TH STREET

American
Indian Center

16TH STREET

280

Central
Basin

BUENA
VISTA

Mission
Dolores

CASTRO

MISSION

POTRERO
HILL

SOUTHERN EMBARCADERO FREEWAY

3RD STREET

EUREKA
VALLEY

CASTRO STREET

DOLORES STREET

GUERRERO STREET

MISSION STREET

San Francisco
General Hospital

Twin
Peaks

CLIPPER STREET

CEASER CHAVEZ ST

JAMES LICK FREEWAY

ST
L

NOE VALLEY

DIAMOND HEIGHTS
Glen Canyon
Park

BERNAL
HEIGHTS

101

India
Basin

ORTOLA DRIVE

Mt Davidson
282m

SAN JOSE AVENUE

BAYSHORE

RANCIS
OOD

GLEN PARK

280

QUINT STREET

City College of
San Francisco

N AVENUE

Balboa
Park

MISSION STREET

PORTOLA

EXCELSIOR

3RD STREET

JAMES LICK FREEWAY

BAYVIEW

LESIDE

PERSIA AVENUE

John McLaren

MANSELL STREET

HUNTERS
POINT

OCEAN
IEW

Park

GENEVA AVENUE

101

Candlestick Park Stadium
(SF Giants & 49 'ers)

San Francisco City Limit

San Francisco International Airport

VISITACION
VALLEY
Cow Palace

Chinatown

This is the largest Chinese settlement outside Asia, and it is almost a city in its own right. The Chinese population in San Francisco is now over 150,000 and growing. Immigration started during the gold-rush days when Chinese railway workers were brought over to construct the Transcontinental Railway. They were segregated into a ghetto which became known as Chinatown in the 1850s.

A little bit of China in the heart of America

Today the Chinese population spreads way beyond the 24-city-block area of Chinatown and only a quarter of the city's Chinese population live there. However, Chinatown is still the true cultural and political focus of the community.

Grant Avenue forms the main street, and you enter through a gateway on Bush Street guarded by stone lions. It is the oldest street in the city and is always busy and congested, as you would expect for the most densely populated neighbourhood in San Francisco. Shops filled with cheap oriental souvenirs rub shoulders with restaurants, jade merchants, herb shops and fortune cookie factories.

To see the real Chinatown leave Grant Avenue and wander down some of the side streets, up on to **Stockton Street** and down to **Portsmouth Square**. The area is very safe and there is no need to be concerned by the oppressive crowds. Culturally, this is really a part of China. You will rarely hear English spoken and Caucasians stick out like sore thumbs. Chinatown is not a tourist theme park, it is the real thing.

To see where the Chinese shop, wander along Stockton Street any morning and join the shoppers hunting for the freshest exotic vegetables or maybe buying a live chicken from a stall on the street. Stroll through Portsmouth Square at any time of day and watch the old men playing *mah-jong* and chess. In the early morning this is a popular place to practise *tai chi* exercises.

All this exotic colour cries out to be photographed, but be careful. Many of the people here strongly dislike having their photograph taken, and while you will not be in any physical danger, the verbal abuse can be awesome.

There are two small museums that can help put Chinatown into historical perspective. **The Chinese Historical Society of America** documents the history of the Chinese in California. It claims to have the largest collection of Chinese American artefacts in the country (*650 Commercial St, tel: (415) 391 1188, open: Wed–Sun noon–4pm, free admission*). **The Chinese Cultural Center**, located on the third floor of the Chinatown Holiday Inn, has regular exhibits of Chinese art and a few permanent cultural exhibits (*750 Kearny St, tel: (415) 986 1822, open: Tue–Sat 10am–4pm, free admission*).

A few temples remain that are worth a visit. The most important is the **Tien Hou Temple** on the top floor of 125 Waverly Street which dates back to the Gold Rush days.

The only way to experience Chinatown is on foot, and lecturers from the Chinese Cultural Center lead a 1–2-hour Chinese Heritage walking tour. A culinary tour is also offered by Wok Wiz Tours (*tel: (650) 355 9657 for details*). Several other walking tours are available. Check with the Visitor Information Center (*900 Market St*) for details.

Pedestrians in Chinatown's Washington Street

Tour: 49-Mile Drive

If you only have one day to see San Francisco then take this drive. It passes virtually every major sight in the city. Where you start is not important, though it is better to plan the drive so that you avoid the congested downtown area during rush hours.

Allow 4 hours.

The route is very well marked with '49-Mile Drive' blue-and-white seagull signs, so it is difficult to get lost.

From Union Square take Post St to Grant Ave, turn left and drive through the Chinatown Gate to California St.

1 Chinatown

The junction of California and Grant is the heart of Chinatown. Cable cars run along this section of California Street – remember they always have right of way.

Continue up to Nob Hill, pass between the Mark Hopkin's Hotel on the left and the Fairmont on the right. Continue past the Flood Mansion and turn right in front of Grace Cathedral on to Taylor St. Turn right on to Washington St and the Cable Car Barn is on the left at the junction with Mason St. Follow the signs as far as Kearny St.

2 Portsmouth Square

A lift from the car park goes straight into Portsmouth Square. This is the social centre of Chinatown.
Turn left on to Kearny, follow the signs through North Beach as far as Lombard St, and turn left. Coit Tower is a short detour to the right. Follow the signs, pass Pier 39 and drive along Fisherman's Wharf to Ghiradelli Square. Take Bay St to Marina Blvd.

3 Fort Mason

This collection of old warehouses and wharves is now home to over 50 non-profit organisations, including Greenpeace, and three small museums: the Mexican Museum, the Museo Italio–Americano and the San Francisco Craft and Folk Art Museum. The SS *Jeremiah O'Brien* is also moored here.
Follow the signs through the Marina District, pass the Palace of Fine Arts and enter the Presidio on Lincoln Blvd.

4 The Presidio

Established by the Spanish in 1776 and taken over by the United States in 1846, these 583 hectares (1,440 acres) of wooded hills are an army base. The drive passes the Presidio Army Museum, protected by antique cannon and housing a collection of military uniforms and weapons.
Continue on Lincoln Blvd and turn off at Long Ave.

5 Fort Point

At the end of the road nestling under the Golden Gate Bridge is Fort Point, the only brick fort west of the Mississippi.
Return to Lincoln Blvd and continue to the end. In Lincoln Park pass the California Palace of the Legion of Honor and turn right on Point Lobos Ave.

6 Cliff House

The Cliff House has restaurants, shops and great views of Seal Rock. The newly renovated building offers a variety of dining experiences with spectacular ocean views.
The road passes the wide expanse of Ocean Beach and hugs the coast until it passes the Zoo on the left, and continues around Lake Merced where it turns north and follows Sunset Blvd to Golden Gate Park. Follow the signs on the meandering route through the park and climb up to the summit of Twin Peaks.

7 Twin Peaks

The 277m (910ft) summit offers a 360-degree panorama of San Francisco.
Continue down across Market St to Dolores St. Pass Mission Dolores on the right and continue through the Mission District to Potrero Hill. Take Highway 280 north to the 6th St exit. Follow Howard St to the Embarcadero Center and follow the signs through the Financial District down Market St to the Civic Center, on to Japantown and return to Union Square down Post St.

Civic Centre

Sitting in the triangle formed by the arteries of Van Ness Avenue and Market Street, this assembly of administrative offices, arts venues and public spaces reflects the civic zeal that erupted after the 1906 earthquake.

Asian Art Museum

The former San Francisco Public Library has been transformed into a museum dedicated to Oriental art. Based on the 12,000-piece collection of former Olympic Committee president Avery Brundage covering 6,000 years,

San Francisco downtown

2,500 objects are on display at any time. There is a remarkable collection of Buddhist art from India, Tibet and Nepal; magnificent examples of Chinese laquer-work and ebony carving; and the largest collection of jade in the western hemisphere with over 1,200 pieces.
200 Larkin St. Tel: (415) 581 3500. www. asianart.org. Open: Tue–Sun 10am–5pm. Closed on major holidays. Admission charge.

City Hall

Designed by Arthur Brown Jr and John Bakewell Jr in 1915, City Hall epitomises the vogue for the Beaux-Arts style rampant at that time. Its baroque dome is modelled on St Peter's in Rome. The parade of allegorical sculpture on the pediment above the Polk Street entrance is by the French artist Henri Crenier. Its figures depict notions like the Wealth of California, Trade and Navigation.

Civic Center Plaza

This tree-lined plaza in front of City Hall sometimes becomes an animated protest arena, but the area has developed a seedy reputation. It is now a refuge for the homeless and the whole area has become a gathering place for panhandlers and alcoholics.

Louise M Davies Symphony Hall

This ultramodern glass and granite building has been the home of the San Francisco Symphony since 1980. Inside the hall is a 9,235-pipe organ, the largest concert-hall organ in North America. Outside, a Henry Moore reclining figure complements the modern exterior.
Van Ness Ave & Grove St. Tel: (415) 552 8338. www.sfsymphony.org. Tours are

offered every half-hour Mon & Wed 10am–2.30pm. Admission charge.

San Francisco Main Library

Built in 1996, this brilliant-white building, designed by architect I M Pei, replaced the original 1917 library building damaged in the 1989 Loma Prieta earthquake.
100 Larkin St at Grove St. Tel: (415) 557 4400, http://sfpl.lib.ca.us. Library open: Tue–Thur 9am–8pm, Fri noon–6pm, Sat 10am–6pm, Sun noon–5pm, Mon 10am–6pm. Free admission.

United Nations Plaza

East of Hyde Street stands the Federal Building, and beside it the United Nations Plaza with an equestrian statue of Simón Bolivar, the liberator of South America. The name of the plaza commemorates the signing of the UN Charter in 1945 in the nearby War Memorial Opera House. The Heart of the City Farmers' Market takes place here every Wednesday and Sunday.
Polk and McAllister Sts.

The War Memorial Opera House

The San Francisco Opera moved to this grand neoclassical building in 1923. The city is well known for its tradition of fine opera, and the great Enrico Caruso sang here the night before the 1906 earthquake.

The Opera House is shared with America's oldest professional ballet company, the San Francisco Ballet.
*Van Ness Ave & Grove St.
Tel: (415) 861 4008. www.sfopera.com. Tours are offered every half-hour Mon only, 10am–2.30pm. Admission charge.*

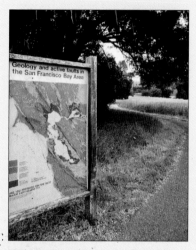

The catastrophic events of 1906 linger in the minds of visitors to the Golden State, but Californian residents rarely think about earthquakes – until a big one happens. Fortunately this is not a common occurrence, though rather more common than a lot of Californians would like to believe.

Eighty per cent of the population lives on a series of fault lines that include the infamous San Andreas Fault. Earthquakes of varying magnitude are common throughout the state but they are usually too minor to feel, never mind cause damage.

Charles Richter at the California Institute of Technology devised the measurement of energy released by an earthquake in the 1940s. The scale is logarithmic, with each number on the scale representing a ten-fold increase in ground vibration. Since 1980, 24 earthquakes with a magnitude of 5.5 and above have caused several billion dollars' worth of damage in the state. The biggest was the Loma Prieta that shook the San Francisco Bay area with a 7.1 magnitude jolt in 1989, resulting in 63 deaths, 3,757 injuries and a $5.9 billion bill. It was the worst disaster for San Francisco since the great earthquake and fire of 1906.

An earthquake happens when the earth's tectonic plates, which are continually sliding past each other, meet an obstruction which causes a building up of tension that is suddenly released. The San Andreas Fault lies along the junction of the Pacific plate and North American plate which move past each other at about two inches a year. In 1906, the release of tension along this fault created an earthquake that measured 8.3 on the Richter scale and devastated San Francisco.

The San Andreas Fault runs from the Imperial Valley in the southeast of the state to Mendocino on the northern coast, and the whole state is crisscrossed by a multitude of lesser fault lines. Every day hundreds of small quakes shake seismographs but barely make a ripple in a glass of water.

The best place to see the San Andreas Fault is 48km (30 miles) north of San Francisco at Point Reyes. The National Park Service has developed an earthquake trail where visitors can actually walk along the San Andreas fault line and witness the magnitude of the 1906 disaster.

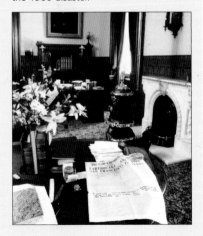

Facing page above: earthquake trail near the Bear Valley Visitors Center, Point Reyes National Seashore, just north of San Francisco; below: seismograph recording earthquakes
Above: Point Reyes, where you can see the San Andreas Fault; right: 1906 newspapers with San Francisco earthquake headlines and articles on display in restored State Governor's Office, state capitol building, Sacramento

Coit Tower

The tower was built as a memorial to volunteer firemen with a bequest from Lillie Hitchcock Coit, a 19th-century eccentric who chased fire engines. Popular opinion has it that the tower was designed to look like the nozzle of a hose. The Pioneer Park car parking area below the tower gives good views of the bay. Even better, take a lift to the observation deck at the top of the tower.

Inside are 16 murals that are the work of 25 painters who created them as part of a make-work project during the 1930s depression. They are masterpieces of social realism depicting the lives of Californian labourers.

Telegraph Hill, San Francisco. Tel: (415) 362 0808. www.coittower.org. Open: daily 10am–4.30pm. Admission charge.

The Financial District

As its name implies, this is the major commercial centre of San Francisco.

Bank of America

The massive, black structure of the bank towers over most of the other buildings in the area. A bird's-eye view of the city can be had from the Carnelian Room restaurant and bar on the 52nd floor.

At the other end of the building, on the concourse, are two art galleries. Both show the work of noted local artists.

555 California St, San Francisco. Tel: (415) 433 7500. Galleries are open daily.

The Embarcadero Center

The most distinctive group of buildings in the Financial District, they house a three-level shopping mall, offices and some major hotels.

Parking here is extremely expensive and difficult to find, but there is usually space available in the underground car parking areas at the Embarcadero Center. Even better, with validation from one of the Center's shops, which could be as little as buying a coffee, you can park for up to three hours for less than the cost of a meter.

Ferry Building Marketplace

The landmark clock tower withstood the 1906 earthquake and now the newly renovated Ferry Building has become the city's Mecca for foodies. There are gourmet shops and restaurants inside and a regular farmers' market outside.

The Embarcadero at Market Street. www.ferrybuildingmarketplace.com. Open daily, hours vary.

The Pacific Heritage Museum of the Bank of Canton

This small museum focuses on the contributions that Pacific Rim immigrants have made to the state. The building is located on the site of San Francisco's original mint. Now carefully restored, it has a basement exhibit showing the original vaults of the mint.

608 Commercial St, San Francisco. Tel: (415) 399 1124. www.ibankunited.com/phm. Open: Mon–Fri 10am–4pm. Free admission.

The Wells Fargo History Museum

Full of memorabilia from the early days of the company, including a restored, nine-passenger stagecoach, the main

theme of the museum is the Gold Rush and Wells Fargo's participation.
420 Montgomery St, San Francisco. Tel: (415) 396 2619. www.wellsfargohistory.com/museums/sfmuseum. Open: weekdays 9am–5pm. Free admission.

Fisherman's Wharf

Native San Franciscans dismiss Fisherman's Wharf as one big tourist trap. They may be right, but if you can overlook the amusement arcade, museums and plethora of T-shirt and sea shell jewellery shops, there are still a few authentic corners.

A small fishing fleet still operates out of the harbour at the foot of Jones Street. Their catch is sold to the local restaurants, and at the junction of Jefferson and Taylor streets old Italian families still operate crab stands selling freshly cooked Dungeness crab and sourdough bread. For the old flavour of this part of town, walk along Pier 45, which is still a working wharf.

San Francisco Maritime National Historical Park

Down the street is Hyde Street Pier, part of the National Maritime Museum. Several historic ships are anchored here.
2905 Hyde St, San Francisco. Tel: (415) 556 1843. www.nps.gov/safr. Open: daily 9.30am–5pm (4.30pm in winter). Admission charge.

National Maritime Museum

The nearby National Maritime Museum displays model ships, photographs and various nautical memorabilia.
Beach and Polk Sts, San Francisco.

Tel: (415) 556 1843. www.nps.gov/safr. Open: daily 10am–5pm. Free admission.

Shopping complexes

Both **The Cannery** and **Ghirardelli Square** are shopping complexes worthy of attention. Ghirardelli Square is the original home of Ghirardelli chocolate, which is highly regarded in the US. You can still see the antique chocolate machines working, and even sample the goods. (*See also pp148–51.*)
Ghirardelli Square, 900 North Point St, San Francisco. Tel: (415) 775 5500. www.ghirardellisq.com

Golden Gate Bridge

The Golden Gate was named by John C Frémont in 1846 after the Golden Horn of Constantinople, three years before the Gold Rush. At 2.7km (1³/₄ miles) long, although it is 50 years old, the bridge is still one of the longest single-span suspension bridges in the world and one of the most beautiful.

Both a bicycle path and a footpath cross the bridge. The walk can get pretty cold, particularly if the fog rolls in, and remember you will have to walk back. There is no public transport to take you. There is a vista point at the northern end of the bridge in Marin County, and the view towards San Francisco is spectacular. Photographers may want to pass under the freeway and drive up to the Marin Headlands for the same dramatic view of the city but with the bridge in the foreground.

The Golden Gate Bridge is the most expensive toll bridge in the country, but the toll is only payable driving into San Francisco.

Walk: San Francisco waterfront

This walk combines some of the best views of the Bay with several major tourist sites, good shopping, street entertainment and great food.

Allow 1½ hours.

Start from the Pier 39 multistorey car park between the Embarcadero and North Point. There is usually space available here, and with validation with a purchase from one of Pier 39's shops or restaurants the parking fee is quite reasonable.

1 Pier 39

This old steamship wharf is now a two-level shopping and restaurant complex. The street performers here provide some of the best free entertainment in town, and the views from the end of the pier are some of the best of the bay. Between

September and May, hundreds of California sea lions can be seen from the viewing area at K Dock.

From Pier 39 continue west along the Embarcadero, keeping as close to the waterfront as possible.

2 USS *Pampanito*

This restored World War II fleet submarine, a veteran of six Pacific patrols, sits at Pier 45. Tours are given daily (*tel: (415) 775 1943; open: Sun–Thur 9am–6pm, Fri & Sat 9am–9pm; admission charge*).

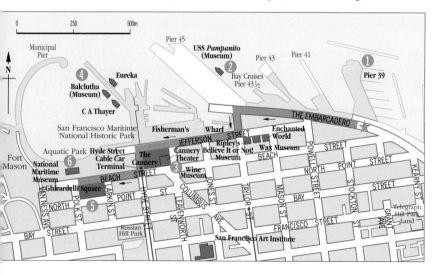

To avoid the main tourist traffic and to experience the old flavour of Fisherman's Wharf, continue along the waterfront by Pier 45, which still has a small working fishing fleet. Return to Jefferson St and continue along to The Cannery on the left-hand side of the street.

3 The Cannery

This multistorey shopping complex was once a fruit and vegetable canning factory for the Del Monte Corporation. During the summer, street performers entertain shoppers in the pleasant central courtyard.

Continue along Jefferson St to Hyde St.

4 Hyde Street Pier

On the right-hand side of the street as it opens out into Aquatic Park is Hyde Street Pier, which is part of the National Maritime Museum. Several historic ships are anchored here including the *Eureka,* an 1890 ferryboat; the *Balclutha,* a Scottish merchant ship built in 1886 that rounded Cape Horn no less than 17 times, carrying coal, wine and hardware from Europe; and a three-masted schooner, *CA Thayer,* that carried timber down the California coast.

The San Francisco Maritime National Historical Park is at 2905 Hyde Street, San Francisco (*tel: (415) 556 1843; open: daily 9.30am–5.30pm, until 4.30pm in the winter; admission charge*).

Walk up Hyde St past the cable-car turntable at the junction with Beach St. Turn right on to Beach and continue past the street vendors selling arts and crafts. There are good views out over Aquatic Park. Continue to Larkin St.

Hyde Street Pier entrance to the San Francisco Maritime National Historical Park, San Francisco

5 Ghirardelli Square

At the junction of Larkin and Beach is one of San Francisco's most attractive shopping and restaurant developments. Ghirardelli Square was originally the home of Ghirardelli chocolate. You can still see the antique chocolate machines working and even sample the goods.

900 North Point St, San Francisco.
Tel: (415) 775 5500.
Return to Beach St and turn left.

6 The National Maritime Museum

Opposite Ghirardelli Square, the National Maritime Museum has a display of model ships, photographs and various nautical memorabilia.

Beach and Polk sts, San Francisco.
Tel: (415) 556 1843. Open: daily 10am–5pm. Free admission.

Return the same way to Pier 39 or take the cable car from the Hyde St terminal.

Golden Gate Park

The 412 hectares (1,017 acres) of parkland that stretch all the way across the western half of San Francisco can be credited to the work of 19th-century horticulturist John McLaren, who turned these acres of rolling sand dunes into one of the great urban parks of the world.

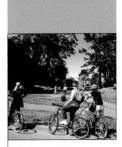
Cyclists watching rollerbladers in Golden Gate Park, San Francisco

This is a major recreation area for the local population. There is a boating lake, a lake for model boats, rhododendron dells, a casting pond for anglers and even a buffalo paddock and a working windmill. At weekends John F Kennedy Drive, the main road through the park, is closed to vehicles and open to jugglers, roller-skaters, skateboarders and anyone else who needs open space and an enthusiastic audience. In addition to the scenic value of the area there are several major attractions.

California Academy of Sciences

The Academy of Sciences is the oldest scientific institution in the west and has been located in Golden Gate Park since 1916. However, the Academy's facility in the park is being completely rebuilt and will be housed in one of the most innovative museum buildings in the world, designed by architect Renzo Piano. The new Academy will open in late 2008.

In the meantime, the Academy has relocated to 875 Howard Street in San Francisco's SOMA District, close to the Moscone Center. Many of the original exhibits have been transferred to this location, including the Steinhart Aquarium which is home to thousands

of tropical fish, reptiles and even penguins.
Tel: (415) 321 8000. www.calacademy.org. Open daily 10am–5pm. Admission charge.

Conservatory of Flowers

This is the oldest building in the park. It was shipped over from London and erected on its present site in 1879. It is a replica of the great conservatory in London's Kew Gardens, and is filled with palms and other tropical plants. *Admission charge.*

Japanese Tea Garden

Adjacent to the Asian Art Museum is the calm and tranquil Japanese Tea Garden, laid out in traditional Japanese style with curved bridges, waterfalls, stone lanterns and a pagoda.
Tel: (415) 752 1171. Open: daily 9am–6pm. Call to check seasonal timings. Admission charge.

MH de Young Memorial Museum

The de Young collection covers European and American paintings up to the 1900s, period furniture, glassware, silverware, and over 600 tribal rugs from central Asia. The building was seriously damaged in the Loma Prieta earthquake and a new state-of-the-art facility

opened in 2005. The building, designed by Herzog & de Meuron of Switzerland, integrates art, architecture and landscape in one multifaceted destination showcasing the museum's priceless collections.
Tel: (415) 863 3330.
www.thinker.org/deyoung. Open: daily 9.30am–5pm. Admission charge.

Strybing Arboretum and Botanical Gardens
This is a 28-hectare (70-acre) park within a park containing over 6,000 species of bushes and trees. There is a Cape Province Garden with South African plants, a New World Cloud Forest and imaginative ideas such as a

Biblical Garden where only plants mentioned in the Bible grow. All the plants are labelled, and the avid horticulturist should be able to find plenty to fully occupy a half-day visit. *Admission charge.*

Marvellous Marin
A short ferry ride from San Francisco's Ferry Building takes you to one of the most spectacularly situated towns in the Bay Area.
Sausalito tumbles down a hillside to an almost Mediterranean corniche, giving unparalleled views of San Francisco. This popular tourist destination has requisite restaurants, expensive shops and art galleries.

Japanese Tea Garden, Golden Gate Park, San Francisco

Grateful Dead mural, Haight-Ashbury

Haight-Ashbury

The name refers to the junction of Haight Street and Ashbury Street, which in the 1960s was to the hippies what North Beach was to the beatniks of the 1950s.

A few psychedelic relics remain. An occasional head shop selling drug-related items still manages to stay in business; antique clothing stores rub shoulders with gay bars and art galleries. You may even see an occasional hippy complete with beads, kaftan and sandals.

Japantown

The area bounded by Geary and Post streets and Laguna and Fillmore streets has become the Japanese equivalent of Chinatown.

Unfortunately it has none of the colour and atmosphere of its Chinese counterpart. **The Japan Center**, a five-acre commercial development that is the heart of Japantown, is an ugly modern series of buildings that says nothing about Japan.

Once you enter the buildings things get better. Although the whole development is a little too bland, the shops do to some extent capture the flavour of Japan. The restaurants most certainly do. Many of the restaurants and sushi bars, both in the Japan Center and the surrounding streets, are totally authentic and serve excellent food.

The **Nihonmachi Mall** on Buchanan Street is one of the pleasant corners of Japantown. You pass under a *torii* gate to a cobblestone pathway that meanders past fountains. On either side of the mall are delightful little shops selling everything from *shojii* screens to antique kimonos. At the end of the mall, across Post Street, stands the five-tiered **Peace Pagoda** designed by the eminent Japanese architect Yoshiro Taniguchi.

Lombard Street

The Crookedest Street in the World winds down from Hyde Street to Leavenworth Street in a series of hairpin bends.

There are spectacular views across to Coit Tower from the top before you plunge down the brick-paved street lined with carefully tended flowerbeds.

Nob Hill

On the high point of the California Street cable-car line, Nob Hill still caters to the elite. This was where the wealthy of San Francisco built their mansions in the mid-1800s, and in 1882 Robert Louis Stevenson described it as 'the hill of palaces'.

Most of these mansions were destroyed by fire following the 1906 earthquake, but one survived. The imposing brownstone mansion of James Flood still sits at the top of the hill and it is now the private Pacific Union Club. Two of the city's grand hotels are neighbours of the Flood Mansion: the Fairmont and, across the road, the Mark Hopkins.

Grace Cathedral sits on Taylor Street opposite the Flood Mansion.

North Beach

This is still a distinctively Italian neighbourhood in spite of recent encroachment by Chinatown.

In the 1950s it was the bohemian centre of San Francisco. Jack Kerouac and other Beat Generation poets would congregate in the Italian coffee bars and in the City Lights Bookstore. The bookstore is still in business on the corner of Columbus Avenue opposite Vesuvio's Bar, another Beatnik haunt, and it remains an important cultural gathering place.

Columbus Avenue is the main street through North Beach and it is crossed by Broadway, which has long had a reputation for its strip joints. A bronze plaque on the wall of the Condor commemorates the building as 'the birthplace of the world's first topless and bottomless entertainment'.

This tawdry strip of cheap sex shows is gradually changing for the better. Even the historic Condor has recently been converted to a pizza parlour.

North of Broadway, around Washington Square, life in Little Italy continues at the steady pace it has always known. Old men sit on benches in the square conversing in Italian, and young men sit in the bars and coffee houses watching the world go by.

North Beach is a great place to relax and escape to Europe for a few hours.

Grace Cathedral atop Nob Hill

San Francisco Museum of Modern Art

This spectacular new museum designed by Mario Botta opened in 1995. The permanent collection includes many works by Clyfford Still, Motherwell, Pollock and Rothko, which are displayed alongside revolving temporary exhibits.

151 3rd St. Tel: (415) 357 4000. www.sfmoma.org. Open: Thur–Tue 10am–6pm (11am in winter). Closed on major holidays. Admission charge.

Palace of Fine Arts

In 1915 the Panama–Pacific Exposition extended all the way across what is now the Marina District. Today there is only one remnant, the Palace of Fine Arts.

The building was designed by the eminent San Francisco architect Bernard Maybeck as a stucco construction, but it deteriorated so severely that in the 1960s it was completely reconstructed in concrete.

More than just a good-looking building, the Palace of Fine Arts houses an auditorium and one of the most entertaining museums in San Francisco.

The **Exploratorium** is a hands-on science museum for children of all ages. Over 600 exhibits wait to be discovered by visitors. *Scientific American* magazine deemed it to be 'the best science museum in the world'.

The Tactile Dome is one of the most popular exhibits in the museum. In this pitch-black sensory chamber, visitors have to feel their way through a maze of passages and textures in total darkness. It is so popular that reservations are required.

The Exploratorium, Marina Blvd & Lyon St. Tel: (415) 561 0307. www.exploratorium.edu. Open: summer, Wed–Sun 10am–5pm (9.30pm on Wed); winter, Wed 1–9.30pm, Thur & Fri 1–5pm, Sat & Sun 10am–5pm. Admission charge. Free on Wed after 6pm.

San Francisco Zoo

The zoo was developed on an area of sand dunes out on Sloat Boulevard close to the Pacific Ocean. Recent renovation has returned the zoo to its position as one of the top six in the US. The collection includes snow leopards, white

VICTORIAN HOUSES

Fine examples of Victorian architecture can be found all over San Francisco, but the view from Alamo Square with the modern city in the background has become an icon of the city. Alamo Square is on Steiner and Fulton streets and late afternoon is the best time to photograph this classic cliché.

On Franklin Street the Haas-Lilienthal House, which was built in 1886, is the only fully furnished Victorian house open to the public. The most unusual is the Octagon House on Gough Street at Union Street. This eight-sided house has been fully restored and tours are available.

Several Victorian houses have now been converted into bed and breakfast establishments.

tigers, pygmy hippos and an excellent gorilla habitat. The new **Primate Discovery Center** has 16 endangered species of monkeys. There is also a separate Children's Zoo where the animals can be both petted and fed.
Sloat Blvd at 45th Ave. Tel: (415) 753 7080. www.sfzoo.org. Open: daily 10am–5pm. Admission charge.

Union Square

If San Francisco has a centre, then this is it. The major department stores are here, and two of the grandest hotels.

The cable cars also go right past the square. The main theatres are around the corner on Geary Street, and all the major airline offices are here.

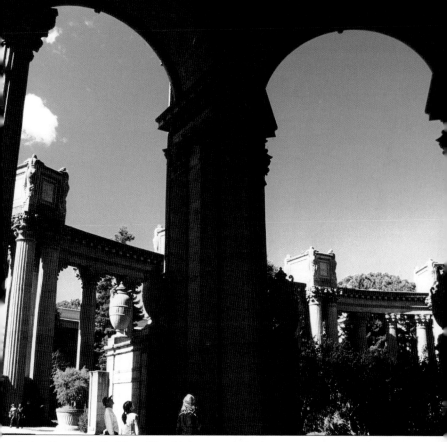

Restored in concrete, the Palace of Fine Arts has a grand rotunda

Walk: downtown San Francisco

San Francisco is one of the few American cities that lends itself to walking. This walk covers the best areas of the commercial, shopping and historic areas of downtown San Francisco.

Allow 2 hours.

Start from Union Square. On the Stockton St side of the Square look for Maiden

Lane. This narrow street has exclusive boutiques and galleries. On the left you will see a Frank Lloyd Wright building that was a model for New York's Guggenheim Museum. Follow Maiden Lane to Kearny St, turn left, walk to Post St and turn right.

1 Crocker Galleria

This glass-domed shopping mall off Montgomery Street was modelled on the Galleria in Milan.
Continue along the canyon of Montgomery St, the Wall Street of the West. This is the financial heart of northern California.

2 Transamerica Pyramid

The unmistakable building on the corner of Montgomery and Washington Streets is the tallest structure in the city at 260m (853ft). The 27th-floor viewing area has been closed for security reasons.
Continue along Montgomery St. Once out of the financial area, the street starts to climb. Continue up the increasingly steep street as far as Vallejo St. There are good views of both the city and the bay.
Turn right and descend to Battery St. Turn left. This is the centre of the

advertising industry and all the major agencies are along here. Continue along Battery to Levi Plaza, the home of Levi Strauss. Opposite is Filbert St.

3 Filbert Street Steps

The steps rise steeply from Battery Street straight up to Coit Tower. The steps are one of the undiscovered treasures of the city. They pass carefully tended gardens and a profusion of flowers during the summer months.

4 Coit Tower

The steps emerge at this distinctive landmark on top of Telegraph Hill. Inside the tower there are wonderful murals painted during the 1930s depicting the workers of San Francisco. The top of the tower gives good views of the city and the bay.

Cable cars and steeply sloping streets epitomise San Francisco

From the tower continue down Filbert St to the Italian North Beach District. Walk as far as Stockton St and turn left. The coffee and garlic aromas of North Beach will give way to smells of Chinatown.

5 Stockton Street

Always busy, Stockton Street is where the Chinese shop. This is the real Chinatown.
Continue along Stockton to Washington St. Turn left and walk one block to Grant Ave. Turn right. Grant is the tourists' Chinatown with gift shops, jewellers and restaurants.

6 Chinatown Gateway

Chinatown ends at this imposing gate, guarded by a pair of dragons.
Turn right on to Sutter St. Here are some of the most fashionable and expensive shops in San Francisco. Walk up Sutter to Powell St. Turn left on Powell and return to Union Square.

Transamerica Pyramid and the Flatiron Sentinel Building

Wine

The first grapevines were introduced to San Diego in 1769 by the Spanish missionaries. The vineyards extended northwards with the establishment of the missions, but it was not until the Gold Rush that wine-making came into its own. The Buena Vista Winery was founded in Sonoma in 1857 and over the next two decades European immigrants built wineries throughout Napa, Sonoma, Santa Clara and the Central Valley.

The industry ground to a halt during 13 years of prohibition and by 1933, when the law was repealed, was in complete disarray.

Techniques and vine stocks improved vastly over the ensuing years so that in the early 1970s California wines could compete with the best in the world.

When a Stag's Leap Wine Cellars' 1973 Cabernet Sauvignon won first place in a blind tasting in Paris, competing against the finest French wines, California wine had truly arrived.

The finest wines are produced from the white Chardonnay grape and the red Cabernet Sauvignon. However, very good wine is produced from virtually every variety of grape including Sauvignon Blanc, Pinot Noir, Chenin Blanc, Riesling, Merlot and California's very own Zinfandel – the Beaujolais of California.

The major wineries extend from Lake County and Mendocino down to the Santa Ynez Valley near Santa Barbara. Napa Valley, a one-hour drive north of San Francisco, is the heart of California wine country and it is here that some of the world's finest wines are produced.

Many of the wineries offer tastings and tours. A guide to the California wineries is available from:
The Wine Institute, 165 Post Street,

San Francisco, California 94108.
Tel: (415) 986 0878.

Facing page above: the tasting room, Sterling Vineyards, Napa Valley
Below: grape harvesting at St Helena
Above: the crop at Pine Ridge Winery, Yountville

Wine country

The wine country begins a mere one-hour drive to the north of San Francisco. Altogether four counties comprise the major wine growing area: Napa, Sonoma, Lake and Mendocino. However, it is Napa Valley that has become synonymous with wine, and many of the finest wines in the world are grown and made here. The Sonoma County wines are often the equal of their Napa neighbours and it was in the historic town of Sonoma that the California wine industry started in the mid-19th century.

St. Francis by Buffano at Robert Mondavi Winery

Napa Valley

There are over 220 wineries in this valley, which is only 48km (30 miles) long and 5km (3 miles) wide.

Most wineries are concentrated along Highway 29 between Napa and Calistoga. Unfortunately, this road also has the greatest concentration of traffic. It is the main road through the valley and during the summer and at weekends it is so busy that the cars can be bumper to bumper all the way.

To avoid this, try the Silverado Trail parallel to Highway 29 (*see p110*).

Most of the wineries offer guided tours and tastings. Several wineries require advance reservations for tours and an increasing number are charging a nominal fee for tastings. The following producers are a few of the highlights.

The Hess Collection Winery

At the southern end of the valley, close to Napa town, the Hess Collection offers a self-guided tour of the winery and a multi-level gallery, with an impressive collection of modern paintings.

4411 Redwood Rd, Napa. Tel: (707) 255 1144. www.hesscollection.com

Domaine Chandon

The tour here covers the manufacture of sparkling wine at one of the valley's few champagne-type wine producers. This modern winery also has one of the area's outstanding restaurants.
California Drive, Yountville.
Tel: (707) 944 2280. www.chandon.com

Rubicon Estate

The magnificent Gothic winery was built in 1879 and is one of the most impressive in the valley. The winery was bought by film director Francis Ford Coppola and now houses an exhibit of Hollywood memorabilia in addition to the expected winery attractions.
1991 St Helena Highway, Rutherford.
Tel: (707) 968 1100.
www.rubiconestate.com

Robert Mondavi Winery

Robert Mondavi has been one of the great innovators in the California wine industry. His collaboration with Baron Rothschild of Bordeaux developed a new breed of Californian wine. The tour covers the whole process of state-of-the-art wine making.

7801 St Helena Highway, Oakville.
Tel: (888) 766 6328.
www.robertmondaviwinery.com

Sterling Vineyards

A cable car transports visitors from the car park to the hilltop winery with wonderful views of the valley.
1111 Dunaweal Lane, Calistoga.
Tel: (800) 726 6136.
www.sterlingvineyards.com

Clos Pegase

This is one of the newest wineries and also one of the most interesting. The spectacular building was designed by eminent American architect Michael Graves, who was the winner of a competition held in collaboration with the San Francisco Museum of Modern Art.

The winery houses the vast art collection of Jan Schrem, the owner.
1060 Dunaweal Lane, Calistoga.
Tel: (707) 942 4981.
www.clospegase.com

Oak wine barrels stacked outside Sterling Vineyards, Napa Valley

Tour: Silverado Trail

This country drive not only avoids the heavy traffic of Highway 29 through Napa Valley but passes through some of the most scenic and unspoiled sections of the California wine country. The Silverado Trail was originally a stagecoach route and even today it has a strong feeling of the past.

Allow 2 hours, including stops.

Travelling north, turn right off Highway 29 at Trancas St in Napa. Follow Trancas for 1.6km (1 mile) and turn left on to the Silverado Trail.

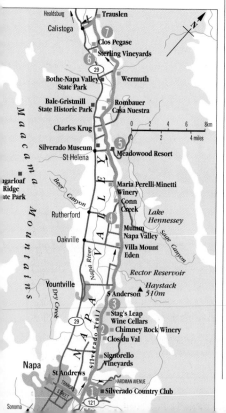

Half a mile along the Silverado Trail turn right on to Hardman Ave. At the end of Hardman turn right and the Silverado Country Club is on the left.

1 Silverado Country Club

This magnificent plantation-style building was originally the 1870 home of General John Miller. It is now one of the finest resort facilities in California with two championship golf courses, 20 tennis courts and two gourmet restaurants. *Return to the Silverado Trail and turn right. Drive for two miles, passing rolling vineyards on both sides of the road.*

2 Chimney Rock Winery

A golf course used to be located on this prime vineyard land. The distinctive Dutch architecture of the winery transports the visitor to the wine country of South Africa. There is a public tasting room and tours by appointment. *Return to the Silverado Trail and turn right. Drive for 1.6km (1 mile).*

3 Stag's Leap Wine Cellars

This is the winery that put Napa Valley on the international wine map in the 1970s, when one of its Cabernet

Sauvignon wines beat the best French wines at a blind tasting in Paris.

The winery has a tasting room open to the public, and tours are available by appointment.

5766 Silverado Trail, Napa.
Tel: (707) 944 2020.
Continue north on the Silverado Trail, passing several small wineries. Mumm Napa Valley is on the left.

4 Mumm Napa Valley

This state-of-the-art winery, owned in part by the great French champagne house, is one of the few producers of champagne-style wines in the valley. Open for both tours and tasting.

8445 Silverado Trail, Rutherford.
Tel: (707) 942 3400.
Drive 3km (2 miles) north to Howell Mountain Rd. Turn right and then immediately left on to a winding lane.

5 Meadowood Resort

Beautifully situated in the midst of a tree-covered valley, the Meadowood Resort provides a secluded retreat with golf, tennis, fine dining and a perfectly manicured croquet lawn.

900 Meadowood Lane, St Helena.
Tel: (800) 458 8080.
The Trail winds north through yet more vineyards. After 6km (4 miles), turn left on to Dunaweal Lane.

6 Sterling Vineyards

An aerial tram transports visitors to this hilltop winery. In addition to the wine, there are magnificent views down the Napa Valley.

1111 Dunaweal Lane, Calistoga.
Tel: (707) 942 5151.

7 Clos Pegase

Directly across the road from Sterling, the controversial architecture of this winery is hard to miss. Inside you will find a very impressive art collection.

1060 Dunaweal Lane, Calistoga.
Tel: (707) 942 4981.
Continue along the Silverado Trail to its end in Calistoga. Turn left into town.

Sterling Vineyards aerial tramway car, Calistoga

Calistoga

At the northern end of the Napa Valley the small town of Calistoga has been an important spa since the mid-1800s.

The natural thermal activity in the area and the profusion of hot springs have resulted in a thriving business in steam baths, mud baths and massage.

Old Faithful of California

This is one of the few geysers in the world that erupts at regular intervals. If you have never seen a geyser, the novelty value may make this attraction worth the nominal entrance fee. A run-down group of buildings is an excuse for an entrance and prevent the geyser being seen from the road.

Behind these buildings is a scrappy piece of waste-land out of which a 30m (100ft) jet of water shoots every 40 minutes.
Tubbs Lane, 2.5km (1¹/₂ miles) north of Calistoga off Highway 29. Open: daily. Admission charge.

St Helena

This charming little town is the hub of Napa Valley and it still looks much the same as it did in the 1890s. This is yet another place

that Robert Louis Stevenson spent a few months in 1880, and the mandatory memorabilia collection is housed in the Silverado Museum wing of the public library. It was in St Helena that he wrote the book *The Silverado Squatters*.

Several wineries are close to town and the Beringer property to the north on Highway 29 is particularly interesting. Spring Mountain Vineyards at 2805 Spring Mountain Road, to the northwest of town, is a popular excursion mainly because of its role as the winery in the television series *Falcon Crest*.

Valley of the Moon

Only a 30-minute drive west from Napa, the Valley of the Moon extends from Sonoma to Santa Rosa. This premium wine-growing region was named by writer Jack London, who made his last home here.

Glen Ellen

The tiny village of Glen Ellen lies to the west of Sonoma on Highway 12 at the southern end of the Valley of the Moon. This sleepy corner of the wine

ROBERT LOUIS STEVENSON

Stevenson was born in Edinburgh in 1850. In 1876 he met and fell in love with a married American woman, Fanny Osborne. She returned to California in 1878 and the following year he decided to join her.

Stevenson was already suffering from severe respiratory problems when he reached California, but he managed to eke out a meagre living in Monterey and San Francisco. His walks along what is now Pebble Beach, Monterey, are thought to have provided material for his popular novel *Treasure Island*.

In 1880 Stevenson married Fanny. Their honeymoon spent near St Helena in the Napa Valley resulted in the book, *The Silverado Squatters*. The couple went to Scotland for a reconciliation with his parents before once more returning to San Francisco en route for the South Pacific. He died in Samoa in 1894.

country is notable as the home of writer Jack London.

Jack London State Park

West of Glen Ellen is the 324-hectare (800-acre) Jack London State Historic Park. The land was London's beloved Beauty Ranch and within the park lie the remains of the Wolf House, destroyed by a mysterious fire before completion in 1913.

After London's death in 1916, his wife Charmian built the House with Happy Walls, now a museum dedicated to London with memorabilia of his travels, particularly in the South Pacific. The park has numerous walking trails and is ideal for picnics.

Open: daily, from dawn to dusk.
Free admission.

Sonoma

The central plaza of Sonoma was laid out by General Vallejo in 1835 and it is surrounded by one of the finest groups of Mexican-era adobe buildings in northern California.

Just off the main plaza, the San Francisco de Solano mission is the most northerly of the chain and was the last to be built in 1823.

Although Napa Valley now wears the wine-makers' crown, it was Sonoma where the industry started. In 1857 Agoston Haraszthy built the Buena Vista Winery at 18,000 Old Winery Road, Sonoma (*tel: (707) 938 1266*). There are tours of the original caves and the grounds are a perfect spot for a summer picnic.

Buena Vista was the first commercial enterprise, but in 1825 padres from the mission planted a huge vineyard near Fourth Street East in Sonoma. In 1904 the Sebastiani family purchased it and they have been operating the winery ever since at 389 Fourth Street East, Sonoma (*tel: (707) 938 5532*).

Beauty Ranch cottage, Jack London State Historic Park

Gold

When James Marshall discovered gold in the millrace of a sawmill in Coloma in 1848, the course of Californian history changed dramatically.

Within a year, thousands of fortune seekers headed west and started the migration that continues even today.

Gold had always been the carrot dangling in front of the explorers of this frontier land, and once its discovery had been made towns mushroomed overnight.

The legacy of this period still survives in the string of towns along Highway 49 from Nevada City down to Mariposa.

'Weekend miners' still go panning in the rivers, and some commercial mines have reopened. It is thought that as much gold as has already been mined is still in the Californian ground.

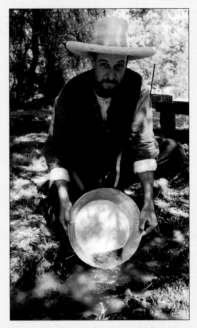

Mine tours are given at the old Empire Mine in Grass Valley, and the North Star Mine has a museum with a vast display of mining equipment.

In the **Malakoff Diggins State Historic Park**, 26km (16 miles) north of Nevada City, you can see an impressive example of landscape erosion as a result of hydraulic mining.

A replica of Sutter's Mill, where gold was discovered, has been constructed on the original site in Coloma. Gold pans are available for rent for anyone wanting to attempt a recreation of the historic event.

Many shops have California gold for sale and there is no shortage of museum exhibits. Perhaps the most impressive display of the immense wealth extracted from the California soil is the $5 million pyramid of gold bars on display at the Old Mint in San Francisco.

Facing page above: living history character William McIntosh pans for gold at Columbia Diggins, Columbia State Historic Park; below: examining a large gold nugget
Right: Boys examining their gold find, Columbia State Historic Park
Below: Gold ore and gold coin, California State Mining and Mineral Museum, Mariposa

Sacramento

Rather than San Francisco or Los Angeles, Sacramento became California's capital city – and appropriately so, since the state's modern history began near here, at a site on the American River. Carpenter James Marshall, sent upstream to construct a new lumbermill by John Sutter, one of Sacramento's first settlers, also discovered gold in the millrace.

Historic bell at Sutters Fort, Sacramento

Sutter's dreams of an agricultural empire were dashed by the 1849 California Gold Rush. Almost overnight his small adobe enclave grew into a commercial centre of well over half a million people. By 1854, Sacramento had become the state capital.

Sacramento is a city at once relaxed and refreshing – except in extreme summer heat when even rose bushes wilt. Most historic sights and other attractions are easily accessible near downtown. At least one local event, the annual Dixieland Jazz Jubilee held over the Memorial Day weekend, is worthy of rescheduling one's holiday. Also worth doing are lunch or dinner cruises aboard paddle-wheel river boats. More ambitious water adventures include weekend delta cruises departing from (and returning to) San Francisco.

The California Capitol

The state's golden-domed Capitol building is Sacramento's stately centrepiece, situated at 10th Street and the Capitol Mall (between L and N Streets). Particularly worth seeing are the separate Senate and Assembly chambers on the second floor, as well as the Capitol Museum in Room 124.

Outside is 16-hectare (40-acre) Capitol Park, an impressive arboretum, and California's Vietnam Veterans Memorial. Free tickets for guided tours (offered daily in summer) are available at the museum office in the Capitol's basement (*tel: (916) 324 0333* for information and to arrange group tours).

The California State Indian Museum and Sutter's Fort

Near the Capitol, the California State Indian Museum offers a fine collection of Native American artefacts and exhibits of California's first citizens whose cultures have been almost obliterated by subsequent history.

Adjacent Sutter's Fort, the valley's first non-native settlement, represents that history. Established in 1839, even here only a few original adobe brick walls survived the raucous rampages of the Gold Rush. The restored fort complex re-creates civilised life in about 1846, and occasional Living History Days demonstrate settlers' survival skills. *California State Indian Museum: 2618 K St, Sacramento. Tel: (916) 324 0971. Sutter's Fort: 2701 L St. Tel: (916) 445*

4422. Museums open: daily 10am–5pm, except major holidays. Free admission.

The Crocker Art Museum

Near Old Sacramento, the Crocker Art Museum is itself a work of art, in the high Italianate Victorian style. The Crocker is also one of the oldest public art museums in the west, noted for its California landscapes and photography. *216 O St, Sacramento. Tel: (916) 264 5423. www.crockerartmuseum.org. Open: Tue & Wed–Sun 10am–5pm and special hours for special events. Free admission.*

The Governor's Mansion

Peculiar in California, and due to pugnacious state politics, is the fact that there is no official governor's residence – not since 1967 when then-Governor Ronald Reagan and family fled this fine old Victorian house, and it became an eclectic public museum.
16th & H Sts. Tel: (916) 323 3047. www.parks.ca.gov/?page_id=498. Open: daily, except major holidays, 10am–4pm for guided tours only. Free admission.

Old Sacramento

At the west end of J Street, Old Sacramento is a colourful 'city' of refurbished buildings of the Gold Rush era and a state historic park in its entirety. Despite the freeway overhead, the ambience is authentic. Many of the shops re-create Sacramento's frontier past as successfully as the superb museums. The **California State Railroad Museum** at 111 I Street (*tel: (916) 445 6645*) has an exceptional collection of restored locomotives and unique old railroad cars, as well as history dioramas and

exhibits. Outdoors, hands-on train enthusiasts enjoy the 40-minute ride on the Sacramento Southern Railroad, and special events such as the National Handcar Races held each September.

Also worthwhile in Old Sacramento is the **Sacramento History Center** at 101 I Street (*tel: (916) 449 2057*). The **BF Hastings Building** at 2nd and J, once the Wells Fargo building and the western end of the Pony Express, also houses (upstairs) the original chambers of the California Supreme Court. The **Big Four Building** at 2nd and Front, the original Central Pacific Railroad headquarters, includes (downstairs) a functional re-creation of the 1880s Huntington & Hopkins Hardware Store. The frame-and-canvas **Old Eagle Theatre** at 925 Front Street offers live period theatre (*tel: (916) 323 6343*).

For almost-authentic fun, take a paddle-wheel river-boat ride aboard the *Matthew McKinley*. The boat departs from the L Street Landing (*tel: (916) 552 2933*). Another river-boat option is the *River City Queen* (*tel: (916) 921 1111*).

Old Sacramento is free, but museums and other attractions charge fees. Most public buildings are open daily, 10am–5pm. Free **Old Sacramento Walking Tours** leave from the train passenger station at Front and J Streets on Saturday and Sunday at 11.30am and 1.30pm (*tel: (916) 443 2274*). For more information about Old Sacramento, contact the Sacramento State Parks Docent Association office (*tel: 916 323 9278*) at the railroad museum, or stop by the Old Sacramento Merchants Association booth at 917 Front Street (*tel: (916) 264 7031*).

Highway 49: gold country

Just as Nevada is known as the Silver State, it is no accident that California became the Golden State. The 1849 California Gold Rush created modern-day California. And the Gold Rush began here, when James Marshall made the first gold discovery, on the western slope of the Sierra Nevada along the 483km (300-mile) stretch of small towns and rolling foothills now loosely connected by Highway 49.

Victorian building in Nevada City

The Spanish myth of *la veta madre* or 'the mother lode' refers to a single rich vein of ore once considered the source of all gold in the territory. Historical purists will point out that the mother lode actually refers only to the territory's southern mines, those from Placerville south. The northern mines, not included under this interpretation of the mother lode, include the areas of Auburn, Grass Valley and Nevada City, as well as the wild and woolly Yuba and Feather River watersheds reaching all the way up to Oroville north of Sacramento.

California's Gold Country is a delightful destination for one-day and weekend excursions. It also warrants much slower exploration. The area offers a number of low-key attractions that include historical museums and parks, boutique wineries and produce stands. For those looking for a quieter getaway there are hiking and cycling treks in some quite outstanding countryside, as well as gold panning, fishing and (in non-drought years) superb white-water river rafting.

The northern mines
Auburn and Coloma
Partly included within the 97-hectare (240-acre) Marshall Gold Discovery State Historic Park (*tel: (530) 622 3470*) 16km (10 miles) south of Auburn, Coloma marks the spot where James Marshall found gold in early 1848. This birthplace of the state's Gold Rush, now a mecca for white-water rafters on the American River's south fork, includes a replica of **Sutter's Mill**, restored historic buildings, an excellent museum, and commercial shops and galleries (*open: 10am–5pm daily*).

The community of Auburn just north is noted for its historic Old Town and the Placer County Courthouse, built entirely of local materials and beautifully restored. Worth more time, though, is the Bernhard House Museum annexe (*tel: (530) 889 6500*), which is completely furnished with Victorian antiques.

Grass Valley
North of Auburn are the twin foothill towns of **Grass Valley** and **Nevada City**, popular getaways for Californians.

Once home to notorious dancer Lola Montez, who scandalised Europe (and eventually even San Francisco), Grass Valley was also home town of Lotta Crabtree – Montez's protegée, the darling of the gold camps, and the first entertainer ever to become a millionaire.

Proud of its venerable **Holbrooke Hotel** and home-made Cornish-style pasties, a predilection passed on by hardrock miners from Cornwall, England, **Cousin Jacks**, Grass Valley's most striking attraction, is the mine they worked in.

Empire Mine State Park at 10791 East Empire Street (*tel: (916) 273 8522*) is a 317-hectare (784-acre) indoor-outdoor museum of mine shafts and ruins, opulent buildings, gracious gardens and interpretive walks and displays. The Empire Mine was one of the richest and oldest hardrock mines in the state when it closed in 1956. Owner William Bourn was one of the richest men in California; here, you can see his family cottage.

Nevada City

Historically, Nevada City has been host to innovators and innovations. World-class soprano Emma Nevada and Andrew Hallidie, inventor of the cable car, were both born here.

Nevada City created new and radical mining techniques, including hydraulic mining. Social engineering was also no surprise: US Senator AJ Sargent, a local resident, prepared legislation which led to American women's suffrage. Meetings held here ultimately established both the University of California and Pacific Gas & Electric, the world's largest utility company.

Noted today for its fine Victorian homes, active arts community, and the historic **National Hotel**, Nevada City's most unusual legacy is actually outside town and quite remote. **Malakoff Diggins State Historic Park** (*tel: (530) 265 2740*) is an oddly enchanting environmental horror, including a massive mine pit with colourful crags and spires created by hydraulic mining in the 1870s. Malakoff also offers good hiking, camping, and the Gold Rush ghost town of North Bloomfield.

Beyond Malakoff Diggins, Highway 49 weaves through rugged Yuba River Canyon past the striking tin-roofed towns of **Downieville** and **Sierra City**, birthplace of the eccentric Gold Rush fraternity of E Clampus Vitus. (The Clampers' ancient motto, 'I believe because it is absurd', speaks truth even in modern-day California.)

Beyond Sierra City is the **Gold Lakes** region and **Plumas-Eureka State Park** (*tel: (530) 836 2380*), where snowbound miners used mining trams as the world's first ski lifts.

Northern mines miscellany
For more information, contact:
Auburn Area Chamber of Commerce
512 Ravine Rd, Auburn, CA 95603.
Tel: (530) 885 5616 or
toll-free 800 433 7575.
Nevada City Chamber of Commerce
132 Main St, Nevada City, CA 95959.
Tel: (530) 265 2692.
Nevada County Chamber of Commerce
248 Mail Street, Grass Valley, CA 95945.
Tel: (530) 273 4667,
toll-free in California, 800 752 6222,
toll-free from other states, 800 521 2075.

The southern mines
Placerville to Jackson
South of Coloma is **Placerville** (also known as Hangtown, due to historic local enthusiasm for gallows justice). These days Placerville is primarily proud of its 24-hectare (60-acre) **Gold Bug Mine** (*tel: (530) 642 5207*) on Bedford Avenue just north of town, America's only city-owned gold mine.

First known as Pokerville, then Puckerville, these days **Plymouth** offers few pleasures except fine regional wineries, including **D'Agostini Winery** (*tel: toll-free 800 722 4849*) northeast of town on Shenandoah Road, the state's fourth-oldest winery and a state historic landmark.

The next stop south is **Drytown**, now mostly a collection of antique shops but once cherished by miners for its 27 saloons. **Jackson** is well worth several hours of exploration, with a side trip east up Highway 88 to both **Chaw'se Indian Grinding Rocks State Park** and the serene Gold Rush town of **Volcano.**

Angels Camp
Past Mokelumne Hill and San Andreas (where Gentleman Black Bart finally went to jail) is the little city of **Angels Camp**, made famous by Mark Twain's first successful story, *The Celebrated Jumping Frog of Calaveras County.* The roads here were paved in 1928, the same year the community launched its annual Jumping Frog Jubilee (real frogs, rentals available) held in May at the frogtown fairgrounds south of town.

More interesting year-round, heading east on Highway 4, is **Murphys**, with its odd **Oldtimer's Museum** and the fine

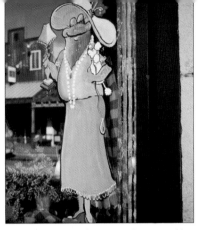

Frog painted on window in Angels Camp, with reflections of old buildings in the window

Murphys Hotel (genuine bullet holes in the doors, wonderful western bar). Nearby are **Mercer Caverns** and **Moaning Cavern** (*see p147*). Up the highway is **Calaveras Big Trees State Park** (*tel: (209) 795 2334*), a few rare groves of Giant Sequoia in a forest featuring good camping and hiking.

Columbia and Sonora
Columbia, the 'Gem of the Southern Mines' 16km (10 miles) south of Angels Camp, is a must-do destination for aficionados of American Westerns. Quite a few, including *High Noon,* were filmed here. The town's authenticity is painstakingly preserved; **Columbia State Historic Park** (*PO Box 151, Columbia, CA 95310, tel: (209) 536 1672. www. columbiacalifornia.com*) offers entire city blocks of oddities – including the state's oldest barber shop – in addition to museums, an exquisite period hotel, saloons, stagecoach rides, and events such as the annual Firemen's Muster in May and June's Columbia Diggins living history weekend. The town is 'open' daily, 9am–5pm, and is a very popular family destination.

Adjacent **Sonora** has its own claims to fame, including historic buildings, fine inns and decent restaurants.

Jamestown

Just south is Jamestown or 'Jimtown', another picturesque city popular with Western film-makers. Downtown features antique and gift shops, plus the opportunity to practise panning for gold in the horse trough outside the livery stable on Main Street (free for children only). But adults can also hunt for riches through **Gold Prospecting Expeditions** (*tel: (209) 984 4653*). Gold mining claims can be rented by the day.

Also fun for families is **Railtown 1897 State Historic Park** (*PO Box 1250 Jamestown, CA 95327, tel: (203) 984 3953*). This 9-hectare (23-acre) park offers picnic grounds and an open-air collection of old railroad cars, plus tours of the old Sierra Railroad Company roundhouse (admission charge) and various steam-powered train tours.

Coulterville

Some 32km (20 miles) south is Coulterville, a refreshing rural community almost unperturbed by progress. A state historic landmark in its entirety, Coulterville offers blocks of boarded-up buildings of the Gold Rush period.

Worth an indoor stroll is Coulterville's **Northern Mariposa County History Center** (*tel: (209) 878 3015*), a crumbling stone museum complete with rifles, gold scales, and Victorian memorabilia from *High Noon*. Across the highway is the **Jeffrey Hotel** and adjacent **Magnolia Saloon**, with swing doors, musty

memorabilia, and even a wooden Indian. The park hosts community events like the annual Coyote Howl and Gunfighters Rendezvous.

Bear Valley to Mariposa

From Coulterville, take the back-roads route into Yosemite National Park or dive down into Merced River Canyon on the loneliest, most treacherous stretch of Highway 49. The latter journey passes what remains of **Bear Valley**, one-time headquarters for the troubled mining empire of explorer John C Frémont, also California's first US senator.

Southernmost of the major gold camps is **Mariposa** ('butterfly' in Spanish). Just off Highway 140 at Jessie and 12th streets is the **Mariposa County History Center** (*tel: (209) 966 2924*), an excellent free museum housed in the local library. The white-pine county courthouse on Bullion Street features the original floor and a good mineral collection. But the local crown jewels are out at the fairgrounds, where the **California Mineral Exhibit** includes very fine samples of the state's natural mineral wealth (*tel: (209) 742 7625*).

Southern mines miscellany
For more information, contact:
El Dorado County Chamber of Commerce
524 Main St, Placerville,
CA 95667. Tel: (916) 621 5885.
Amador County Chamber of Commerce
PO Box 596, Jackson, CA 95642.
Tel: (209) 223 0350.
Calaveras County Visitors Bureau
PO Box 637. Angels Camp, CA 95222
Tel: (800) 225 3764. www.visitcalaveras.org
Tuolumne County Visitors Bureau
PO Box 4020, Sonora, CA 95370. Tel: (800)
446 1333. www.thegreatunfenced.com

Lake Tahoe and environs

'The fairest picture the whole affords', according to Mark Twain, Lake Tahoe in the Sierra Nevada is North America's largest alpine lake: 35km (22 miles) long and 19km (12 miles) across, with a 116-km (72-mile) shoreline. But its size is not its biggest attraction. Its beauty is partially due to the incredible clarity of the cold lake water, almost as pure as distilled water. Peculiar is the fact that Lake Tahoe never freezes, due to the lake's great depth. Beloved by Californians, Tahoe's shoreline is largely privately owned.

Enjoying the Lake Tahoe shoreline

Travellers, however, can enjoy the lake itself at popular public parks. The Tahoe area also offers some of the finest skiing in North America and trails into several spectacular Sierra Nevada wilderness areas. Near Tahoe are other fascinations, including the tiny town of Truckee, where Charlie Chaplin filmed *The Gold Rush*. Since Lake Tahoe straddles the California–Nevada border, the glitter of Nevada's gambling casinos, particularly Reno and Carson City, the Nevada state capital, is also an attraction.

Tahoe area parks

Near Truckee just off I-80 north of Tahoe is **Donner Memorial State Park** (*tel: (530) 582 7892*), where an excellent museum and various artefacts tell the grisly tale of California's notorious Donner Party. A wagon train was trapped here in 1846–7 by winter snows, and the pioneer survivors were eventually reduced to cannibalism.

North of Tahoe City on Highway 28 is **Burton Creek State Park**, good for forest hikes, in addition to (on the lake) small

Tahoe State Recreation Area, popular for its beaches. In **Tahoe City** on West Lake Boulevard is **Gatekeeper's Museum State Park** (*tel: (530) 583 1762*), several acres with picnic areas surrounding a museum emphasising the area's native cultures and natural history.

Centrepiece of **Sugar Pine Point State Park** south of Tahoe City is the 1903 **Ehrmann Mansion**, an elegant fortress built of fine wood and stone, part of San Francisco banker Isaias W Hellman's summer estate. The rocky lakeshore offers sunbathing and strolling. The park is also popular for picnicking and short treks, including a walk to the lake's only operational lighthouse.

Contiguous **DL Bliss** and **Emerald Bay State Parks** further south are popular for camping, hiking, swimming, sunbathing and boating. It is an ambitious shoreline trek from the beaches at DL Bliss to Emerald Bay. Shorter (at least on the way down) and well worth the effort is the 1.6-km (1-mile) Emerald Bay hike to **Vikingsholm**, a massive Scandinavian summer home built in the late 1920s at a cost of half-a-million dollars (tours are offered in summer). Another way to get to Vikingsholm and its fjord-like bay is by boat – a very big boat, a stern-wheeler, with tours departing from South Lake Tahoe (*tel: (530) 525 7277*); dance cruises are also available.

Near the south shore beaches and Camp Richardson is the **Pope-Baldwin Recreation Area**, which includes the **Tallac Historic Site.** Here 19 historic summer homes (some fully restored) testify to Tahoe's past as the playground for California's rich and powerful. Exhibits in the **Tallac Museum** (inside Lucky Baldwin's Baldwin Estate) tell the story, or take a guided tour (summer only). Special events here include Sunday Chamber music, a bluegrass festival in August, and the weekend Starlight Jazz Festival (usually August into September).

Lake Tahoe was 'discovered' internationally when the 1960 Winter Olympics were held at **Squaw Valley.** Some decades later, though there are many others, skiers and non-skiers alike still make the pilgrimage to Squaw Valley, even in the summer, just to take the tram for some breathtaking high-altitude views.

Tahoe area miscellany
For more information about the Tahoe area, contact:
Lake Tahoe Visitors Authority Inc
1156 Ski Run Blvd., South Lake Tahoe, CA 96150. Tel: (530) 583 3494, toll-free in California, 800 288 2463, toll-free from out of state, 800 824 5150.
www.virtualtahoe.com
Tahoe North Visitors and Convention Bureau
PO Box 5578 (850 N. Lake Blvd.), Tahoe City, CA 95730. Tel: toll-free in California, 800 822 5959, toll-free from out of state 800 824 8557.
Truckee-Donner Chamber of Commerce
PO Box 2757 (office inside the train station), Truckee, CA 95734. Tel: (530) 587 2757.
www.truckee.com

For parks information, contact:
Sierra State Parks
PO Drawer D, Tanoma, CA 95733. Tel: (530) 525 7232.
The Tahoe Tallac Association
PO Box 1595, South Lake Tahoe, CA 95707. Tel: (530) 541 4975.
US Forest Service Lake Tahoe
PO Box 8465, South Lake Tahoe, CA 95731. Tel: (530) 537 2600.

Spectacular scenery at Lake Tahoe

The High Sierra

The Sierra Nevada is California's most impressive natural feature. This massive granite mountain range is approximately 724km (450 miles) long, starting in the north near Mount Lassen and ending in the desert near the Tehachapi Mountains, and 97–129km (60–80 miles) wide. Some 200 million years old, it was created by volcanic activity. The dramatic peaks and valleys of the Sierra Nevada, however, were jolted into position by earthquake faulting, and then sculpted and scoured smooth by relentless glaciers during the last million years.

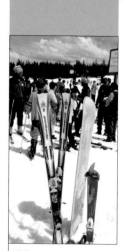

Skiing at Boreal Ridge near Lake Tahoe

Technically, the High Sierra refers to the 241-km (150-mile) long portion of peaks, highlands and icy lakes above the tree line from north of Yosemite Valley south to Cottonwood Pass. In everyday usage, however, the term tends to include the entire range except the almost-urbanised areas of Lake Tahoe, and Yosemite Valley. However the High Sierra is defined, its elegant elevations are most easily appreciated from the range's steep eastern ascent. Mount Whitney near Lone Pine, surrounded by similarly sized sister peaks, is the tallest mountain in continental US (outside Alaska), reaching to 4,418m (14,494ft) above sea level.

SOUTH FROM TAHOE

Highway 89 south from Tahoe leads into California's own big sky country, virtually inaccessible in winter except for highways serving major ski areas. Every highway pass across the Sierra Nevada has its attractions: wilderness access for backpacking, mountain lakes and rivers, family campgrounds, isolated ski resorts and odd old hotels and lodges, vast dark forests and aspens fiery with autumn colour.

The busy Highway 50 route to the valley over **Echo Pass** features some fine scenery, as does the one-time Pony Express route (Highway 88) west over **Carson Pass** and Highway 4 over **Ebbetts Pass**. Thrilling, however, is **Sonora Pass**: Highway 108 climbs to the summit in a single-lane switchback like a goat path, then suddenly slides down the other side (no trailers or recreational vehicles).

Still more spectacular is Highway 395 along the eastern slope of the **Sierra Nevada**, reached from Tahoe via Highway 89. Along the way is minuscule **Markleeville** and its unusual Cutthroat Saloon. Just west of town is the worthwhile **Grover Hot Springs State Park** (*tel: (530) 694 2248*), quite popular for its public hot and cold spring-fed pools, open year-round except two weeks in September.

Bodie

The one-time gold-mining boom town of Bodie is California's largest ghost town, an evocative and ramshackle collection of woodframe buildings now protected as a state historic park. North of Mono Lake and reached via Highways 395 and 270 (Bodie Road), Bodie is a must-see destination.

What remains of what was once one of the wildest mining camps in the west (famous for its wicked citizens, worse weather, wide streets and bad whiskey) offers absolutely non-commercial witness to the desolation of frontier life. Preserved in a state of 'arrested decay', Bodie self-guided walking tours allow visitors to peer into the weathered homes, saloons, stores, restaurants and livery stables that populate this half-day's exploration. Bring water and a picnic lunch (no services available).

The town is 'open' 9am–7pm in summer, until 4pm the rest of the year (only the truly intrepid try to visit Bodie when the town is buried under winter snowdrifts).

Bodie State Historic Park, PO Box 515, Bridgeport, CA 93517.
Tel: (760) 647 6445.

Mammoth Lakes

Noted primarily as a resort centre popular with southern California skiers, the Mammoth Lakes area also offers a respite from eastern Sierra Nevada sagebrush in the form of forests, hot springs and geological oddities along area trails. Most famous here is Devil's Postpile, a fascinating collection of vertical basalt columns formed by slow-cooling lava flows. Officially 'not recommended' by the US Forest Service for swimming or soaking, **Hot Creek** is none the less an immensely popular public hot springs 5km (3 miles) off Highway 395 via Long Valley Airport Road.

Mammoth Lakes Visitor Information Center: Highway 203, PO Box 48, Mammoth Lakes, CA 93546.
Tel: (760) 934 2712. www. visitmammoth.com. Open: daily sunrise to sunset. Free admission.

Early winter dawn in the High Sierra

Mono Lake

Once known as the Dead Sea of California, million-year-old Mono Lake is a large alkaline inland sea on the high plateau east of Yosemite. Far from 'dead', however, Mono Lake is home during at least part of each year to over 300 bird species, including almost the entire breeding population of California gulls. The saline waters here make even the worst of swimmers almost unsinkable.

Most striking, though, are Mono Lake's vast, surrounding salt flats and unusual formation of tufa – freeform pillars of calcium carbonate (limestone) originally created underwater where calcium-rich fresh spring water flowed into the salty lake. These 200- to 900-year-old bone-white spires are now exposed to view, due to Los Angeles's thirst for new urban water sources. Since 1941, when Mono Lake's feeder streams were first tapped, the lake level has dropped more than 14m (45ft).

The best place to explore Mono Lake's tufa collection is the **South Tufa Area** off Highway 120. Nearby are some interesting volcanic formations including Mono Craters, Panum Crater and Devil's Punchbowl. For more information, contact the New Mono Lake Visitor Center in Lee Vining (*tel: (760) 647 6595. www.monolake.org*).

Sequoia and Kings Canyon National Parks

Even when Yosemite National Park is as packed with people as a suburban shopping mall, Kings Canyon and Sequoia National Parks to the south are relatively unruffled. Contiguous and equal to each other in grandeur, Kings Canyon primarily pays homage to the High Sierra wilderness of Kings River country, while Sequoia shows off its stands of Giant Sequoia. Though Kings Canyon has big trees, accessible from campground trails, those at Sequoia's Giant Forest are incomparable. The everyday big tree measures 3–4.5m (10–15ft) across and stands about 76m (250ft) tall, but the giants are awesome

Tufa towers, Mono Lake

indeed. The lowest limb of the 'General Sherman', for example, is 2m (7ft) across and would create a canopy for a 12-storey building.

For more information about these two exceptional parks, everything from backcountry to natural history lessons (including wildflower hikes), winter snowshoe treks, and Nordic ski touring, contact Box E, Kings Canyon National Park, CA 93633 (tel: (559) 335 2315), or Sequoia National Park, Ash Mountain, PO Box 10, Three Rivers, CA 93271 (tel: (559) 565 3341).

The White Mountains

An all-day journey at best, a side-trip via Highway 168 from Big Pine east to the stark White Mountains and the Bristlecone Pine Forest is worth the effort. Here stand the most ancient living things on earth, scattered groves of gnarled *Pinus longaeva* or bristlecone pine trees. Many of these sturdy, scruffy, and seemingly dead trees are estimated to be more than 4,000 years old. The area is desolate, so start with a full tank of petrol and bring your own water and food (camp grounds available).

White Mountains Ranger Station (US Forest Service), 798 N Main St, Bishop, CA 93514. Tel: (760) 873 2500.

Mount Whitney and environs

Not for solitude do visitors climb to the top of Mount Whitney, highest peak in continental US outside Alaska. During the mid-July to early October snow-free season the 16-km (10-mile) trail to the top can become dangerously overcrowded, so Forest Service permits (available in Lone Pine) are required.

The awesome topography of Kings Canyon

An interesting aside between the mountain and the town is the **Alabama Hills**, a dirt-road detour through enormous granite boulders, perhaps familiar as backdrops for Westerns such as *High Sierra*, *Bad Day at Black Rock* and *They Died With Their Boots On*. More fascinating is the fact that quite close to Mount Whitney, via Highway 136 southeast from Lone Pine, is **Death Valley National Monument**, the lowest point in continental US.

High Sierra miscellany

Local US Forest Service outposts, usually situated along public highways, are the most consistent sources of information for remote areas of the Sierra Nevada. Maps, camping and recreation information, and fire and wilderness permits are available.

For further information, contact:

Alpine County Chamber of Commerce
PO Box 265, Markleeville, CA 96120.
Tel: (530) 694 2475. www.alpinecounty.com
Bishop Chamber of Commerce
PO Box 690, N Main St, Bishop, CA 93514.
Tel: (760) 873 8405. www.bishopvisitor.com
Lone Pine Chamber of Commerce
PO Box 749 (126 S Main), Lone Pine,
CA 93545. Tel: (760) 876 4444.
www.lonepinechamber.com

Trees

'General Sherman' is the largest living thing on earth. He weighs 1,407 tonnes (1,385 tons), measures 31m (103ft) around, 84m (276ft) tall and is about 3,000 years old.

'General Sherman' is a Giant Sequoia. Sequoia National Park in the Sierra Nevada mountains is home to the big trees. The massive conifers that lived when dinosaurs roamed the earth only grow at high altitudes in the mountains of California. Apart from Sequoia, small groves can be seen in Yosemite National Park at Mariposa Grove and Tuolumne Grove and at Calaveras Big Trees State Park in the Gold Country.

By some botanical quirk, California is home for not only the biggest trees in the world but also the oldest and the tallest.

From Monterey to the Oregon border, giant redwoods live in a 48-km (30-mile) wide coastal fog belt. The tallest specimens, reaching heights of over 107m (350ft), and ages of up to 2,000 years, live in the far north near Eureka in Redwood National Park.

Groves of redwoods are never too far away on the northern California coast, and an impressive group of trees lives within a 32-km (20-mile) drive from San Francisco across the Golden Gate Bridge in Muir Woods near Mill Valley. The oldest trees are not much to look at and they grow in an inaccessible, hostile environment above 3,048m (10,000ft) in the White Mountains to the east of Big Pine on Highway 395.

The road climbs up to a barren, windswept, rocky landscape scattered with gnarled old trees that were growing when the Pyramids were being built in Egypt.

In the Schulman Grove of the Bristlecone Pine Forest, trees have been found that are over 4,600 years old.

Above: trunks and foliage of Sequoia redwood trees; below: Coastal redwoods along the Avenue of the Giants, Northern California
Facing page: Coastal redwoods in Navarro State Park

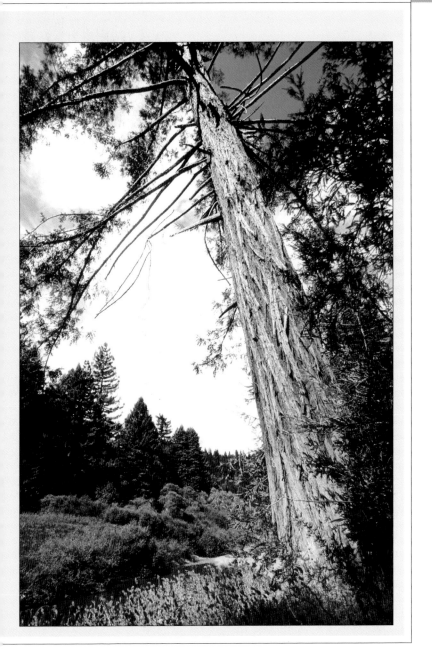

Yosemite

The High Sierra's crowning glory is without doubt glacier-scoured Yosemite National Park. The park was created in 1890 over an area of 3,017sq km (1,165 square miles) that includes the finest valley and high mountain scenery in the US, wildly picturesque with almost vertical walls of granite. Its popularity is confirmed by over three million tourists who visit the park every year and create environmental problems that are a continuing source of controversy.

Yosemite Falls, Yosemite Meadow and cyclist in summer, Yosemite National Park

The heart and soul of the park is the Yosemite Valley. This 11-km (7-mile) long, 1.6-km (1-mile) wide canyon attracts over 80 per cent of all visiting traffic, and in the summer it can be a nightmare. During peak holiday periods every single room and campsite is booked not only in the park but also in the surrounding towns. Reservations are an absolute necessity at these times, and the earlier the better. Paradoxically, car parking space is often available on peak holiday weekends. Local Californians are so used to the madding crowds visiting Yosemite throughout the year that they tend to stay away from the area when they expect the worst congestion.

The reason for all this popularity is apparent as soon as you drive past the entrance stations.

Most people enter Yosemite National Park on Highway 140 from Merced. This is both the shortest and fastest route from I-5 and the San Francisco Bay area. A more dramatic approach is by Highway 120 that eventually becomes the **Tioga Pass**, which at 3,031m (9,945ft) is the highest vehicle pass in

California. Most years heavy snow closes the pass from mid-October to early May.

Whichever way you enter Yosemite, you will eventually want to make your way to the valley. Few places in the world have such a concentration of natural spectacle. Sheer rock walls rise either side of the Merced River almost as soon as you enter the valley proper. Rising 914m (3,000ft) above the valley floor, the giant granite bastion of **El Capitan** is reputedly the biggest monolith on earth. As you drive directly below this massive rock face it is almost impossible to gauge the scale until the insect-like climbers come into view.

Several more imposing towers of rock loom above the 27-km (17-mile) loop road through the valley, including **Sentinal Dome**, **Cathedral Spires** and **The Three Brothers**. The climax of the valley is the distinctive silhouette of **Half Dome** that has become the symbol of the Yosemite Park and Curry Company.

Here in the core of the valley is North America's highest waterfall. The **Yosemite Falls** cascade 739m (2,425ft) to join the Merced River.

In the midst of all this incomparable wilderness is a surprisingly extensive development of accommodation, shops and restaurants. Immediately below Yosemite Falls lies **Yosemite Village**. This is always the busiest place in the whole of Yosemite; the **Yosemite National Park Visitor Center** (*tel: (559) 372 0299*) is here, where wilderness permits can be obtained for overnight camping trips. The area is a hikers' paradise and the centre has a good selection of guide books and trail maps.

The only privately owned property in the park is the Ansel Adams Gallery located between the Visitor Center and the post office. They have an excellent inventory of fine arts and crafts together with books and photographs by some of the world's great photographers, including the legendary Ansel Adams.

Several places in the park give spectacular views. The classic vista is from **Tunnel View** on the road to the awe-inspiring **Mariposa Grove** of Giant Sequoia trees. The road past **Badger Pass**, California's oldest ski resort, leads to **Glacier Point** which, at 2,199m (7,214ft), gives spectacular views.

On the opposite side of the valley, the Tioga Pass Road crosses some of the most beautiful, unspoiled wilderness in the state. **Tenaya Lake** sits at 2,484m (8,149ft), surrounded by huge, polished granite domes. A little further along, the road opens out into **Tuolumne Meadows** before rising to the 3,030m (9,941ft) Tioga Pass.

Yosemite miscellany

One of the great classic hotels of California is the **Ahwahnee** (*tel: (559) 252 4848*) near Yosemite Village. It is often booked for over a year in advance. The spectacular Ahwahnee Dining Room (*tel: (559) 372 1488*) is like an enormous baronial hall with floor-to-ceiling windows overlooking the magnificent scenery of the valley. Jackets and ties are required for dinner.
On the road to Mariposa Grove, the **Wawona Hotel** (*tel: (559) 252 4848*) is like a vision from the Deep South. A nine-hole golf course surrounds the white, colonnaded hotel building.

Skiing at Badger Pass, Yosemite National Park

NORTH FROM TAHOE
Lassen Volcanic National Park

Known to Native Americans as Fire Mountain, Broken Mountain and Mountain-Ripped-Apart, Lassen Peak is the southernmost volcano of the Pacific northwest's vast Cascade Range. Just over an hour's drive east of the valley towns of Chico, Red Bluff or Redding, Lassen Peak today is within a huge caldera formed by the collapse of its mother mountain (Mount Tehama) 30,000 years ago. Lassen is most famous, however, for its much more recent behaviour: surprise volcanic eruptions, culminating in a dramatic 1915 blast of steam and smoke which tossed five-ton boulders into the sky. Lassen's theatrics created such a thrill that this pugnacious peak and its breathtaking setting were protected as a national park in 1916.

Lassen attractions and treks

Unusual at Lassen is its easy access, at least during the few short months when the main road traversing the park (Highway 89) is not blocked by snow. Many of Lassen's features are easily reached from the road, so families with small children and people with physical limitations can enjoy the wilderness.

Some treks can be quite challenging, including the steep, well-graded switchback trail to **Lassen Peak** (start early in the morning; take water and a sweater) and equally impressive **Brokeoff Mountain**. Some visitors try the park's 31-km (19-mile) stretch of the **Pacific Crest Trail**. But for the truly intrepid backpacker, 75 per cent of this 42,897-hectare (106,000-acre) park is preserved as wilderness.

Other Lassen activities

Lassen Park is a volcanic wonderland, featuring three of the world's four types of volcanoes in addition to oddities such as boiling lakes, mudpots and sulphurous steam plumes. The best place to appreciate Lassen's fiery modern-day presence, not to mention summer wildflowers along the way, is at **Bumpass Hell**, where the careless Mr Bumpass lost one of his legs to a boiling mudpot. (Such dangers still exist, so take all warning signs seriously.) Other fairly easy treks include **Paradise Meadows** and **Kings Creek Falls**.

During Lassen's regular 'season', usually from mid-June until October, park rangers offer free campfire talks as well as guided treks. In winter, snowshoe hikes and cross-country ski tours are offered.

Lassen Volcanic National Park, PO Box 100, Mineral, CA 96063. Tel: (530) 595 4444.

Mount Shasta

Shasta is California's mountain masterpiece, the state's sixth-highest peak but more majestic than any other. Lassen's silent sister volcano, about an hour's drive north of Redding via I-5, Shasta stands alone, looming above the ancient lava landscapes and forests. Mount Shasta was one of Sierra Club founder John Muir's favourite places; he first climbed the peak in 1874. Indeed, the mountain's history is mostly one of mountaineering conquest, a feat possible today for any sensible person in reasonably good physical condition.

On an average summer day, 100 or more people attempt the ascent to the summit; about half succeed. (Climbers must register with the Forest Service office in Mount Shasta City before and after the day's efforts.) There are few trails on the mountain, but other treks are enticing. And if Shasta's wilderness areas are too crowded, **Castle Crags State Park**, about 32km (20 miles) south, is usually sublime.

Mount Shasta City at the base of the mountain offers basic services, motels and restaurants. For information about the mountain and town, contact: **Mount Shasta Ranger District**, *204 W Alma Street* (*tel: (530) 926 4511*), and the **Mount Shasta Chamber of Commerce**, *PO Box 201, 300 Pine Street* (*tel: (530) 926 4865*), both in Mount Shasta City, CA 96067.

Halfway between Mount Shasta and Lassen Park via Highway 89 is **McArthur–Burney Falls Memorial State Park**. Teddy Roosevelt extravagantly called Burney Falls 'the Eighth Wonder of the World'. Nearby is very remote **Ahjumawi Lava Springs State Park**, which can only be reached by boat and is home to numerous nesting waterfowl and bald eagles. (For information on both, *tel: (530) 335 2777*.)

Winter recreation

Not famous as a ski resort, Lassen National Park still offers both challenging and family-friendly downhill ski slopes. Almost better, though, are the park's Nordic trails and ranger-guided snowshoe hikes. For more information, contact park headquarters or **Lassen National Forest**
Tel: (530) 258 2141.

For Mount Shasta winter sports information, contact:
Chamber of Commerce
The Ranger District, Castle Lake Nordic Ski Center, PO Box 660, Mt Shasta, CA 96067. Tel: (530) 926 4865.
Mount Shasta Ski Park
104 Siskiyou Ave, Mt Shasta, CA 96067. Tel: (530) 926 8610. www.skipark.com

---

Steam vents in Lassen Volcanic National Park

The north coast

Zigzagging north to the Oregon border from San Francisco's Golden Gate, the remote north coast is perhaps California's greatest treasure. Rolling headlands are common close to San Francisco. But further north the shoreline becomes rugged and rocky, in stark contrast to gentle coastal foothills, and there are great foggy stands of rare coastal redwoods, the tallest trees on earth, along with varied wildlife.

Walking in Muir Woods National Monument, Marin County

Golden Gate National Recreation Area

Though the Golden Gate Bridge and a small coastal strip in San Francisco is included, Golden Gate National Recreation Area (GGNRA) primarily includes the **Marin Headlands** and vast open spaces stretching north to Olema, bordering Point Reyes. Dramatic seacliffs, rolling hills and protected ocean-facing valleys are temptations for serious trekkers.

GGNRA also includes the **Point Bonita Lighthouse**, several former US military installations, the **Marine Mammal Center** (a volunteer-staffed marine wildlife hospital), and the **Marin Headlands Visitor Center**, noted for its science and other educational exhibits. Quite unique and endlessly popular for tours is **Alcatraz Island**, one of America's most famous prisons (*see p84*). *Visitor centres are open daily 8.30am–4.30pm. For more information, contact Golden Gate National Recreation Area, Building 201, Fort Mason, San Francisco, CA 94123. Tel: (415) 561 4700. For Alcatraz tour reservations, tel: (415) 705 5555.*

West Marin parks

Surrounded by the vast acreage of the Golden Gate National Recreation Area are other public and private parks, most of these easily reached from Highway 1. Well known for its fine mountaintop views is **Mount Tamalpais State Park**, which includes **Muir Woods** – an unmissable destination for redwood sightseers.

North of Stinson Beach near serene Bolinas Lagoon is **Audubon Canyon Ranch**, a safe haven for many bird species and a rookery for egrets and great blue herons (nesting sites visible during the March–July nesting season). East of Point Reyes via Sir Francis Drake Boulevard is **Samuel P Taylor State Park**, redwoods and mixed forests with extensive trails and a paved bicycle path. Scattered in sections north of Point Reyes Station and Inverness is **Tomales Bay State Park**, where the sunny and protected inland beaches are the main attraction.

Point Reyes National Monument

Popular in winter for whale-watching, these 26,305 hectares (65,000 acres) of dazzling beaches, coastal dunes, lagoons, marshes and hilltop forests at Point Reyes National Monument in Marin County are perfect for outdoor excursions almost any time of year. Hiking trails extend in all directions; short trails from the **Bear Valley Visitor Center** lead to the US Park Service's **Morgan Horse Ranch** and **Kule Loklo**, a recreation of a typical local Native American community.

The truly imaginative might seek evidence of privateer Sir Francis Drake, after whom the estuary here is named. Historians agree that Drake came ashore at 'a fit and convenient harbour' some-where in California in June 1579. People still search for signs of Drake's treasure, which some believe he jettisoned.

It is a short but many-stepped trip to the **Point Reyes Lighthouse**, known for its astounding views. On a clear day (when the fog lifts), look due south to see the Farallon Islands, a UNESCO Biosphere Reserve and the largest rookery for a great variety of seabirds south of Alaska.

On the way to the Palomarin Trailhead is the **Point Reyes Bird Observatory** (*tel: (415) 868 0655*), established in 1965 as the first such facility in the US. The monument's three visitor centres offer all information, including a schedule of classes and field seminars; or contact Point Reyes National Seashore (*Point Reyes, CA 94956; tel: (415) 663 8132*).

More on Marin parks
For smaller parks in the area contact:
Muir Woods National Monument
Mill Valley, CA 94941. Tel: (415) 389 6957.
Mount Tamalpais State Park
801 Panoramic Highway, Mill Valley, CA 94941. Tel: (415) 388 2070.
For theatre schedule, *tel: (415) 383 0155.*
Audubon Canyon Ranch
4900 Shoreline Highway, Stinson Beach, CA 94970. Tel: (415) 868 9244.
www.egret.org
Samuel P Taylor State Park
PO Box 251, Lagunitas, CA 94952. Tel: (415) 488 9897.
Tomales Bay State Park
Star Route, Inverness, CA 94937. Tel: (415) 669 1140.

North Coast beach at Point Reyes National Seashore

The Sonoma coast

'Spectacular' is the scenic synonym for the Highway 1 tour of the Sonoma County coast. Apparently Alfred Hitchcock agreed, since he chose the coastal village of Bodega Bay to film *The Birds*. Aside from spotting Hitchcock settings, today the area is popular for beachcombing, whale-watching and eating seafood (including local Dungeness crab).

From Bodega Bay north to Jenner are the collected **Sonoma Coast State Beaches**, where the dark and dramatic face of the coast starts to show itself. (Most of the area is not recommended for swimming, and caution is advisable even for tame activities like tidepool exploration. Offshore eddies, undertows, riptides and rogue waves are common.) North of Jenner and the Russian River is reconstructed **Fort Ross State Historic Park** (*open: daily 10am–4.30pm, tel: (707) 847 3286*), established in 1812 as imperial Russia's most distant outpost. Further north, **Salt Point State Park** and **Kruse Rhododendron Preserve** (*tel: (707) 847 3221 for both*) offer more natural attractions in any season (particularly during peak bloom in April or May).

Mendocino, Fort Bragg and environs

The entire town of Mendocino, a tiny woodframe village known for its Cape Cod architecture, is included on the National Register of Historic Places. (To get oriented, start at the Ford House interpretive centre on Main and take the walking tour, *see pp138–9*.) Once a lumber 'dog-hole port' and more recently an artists' enclave, modern-day Mendocino has become a north-coast tourist mecca with abundant small shops. More fascinating is exploring the area's small state parks, starting with **Mendocino Headlands**. For more information, contact Mendocino Area State Parks (*PO Box 440, Mendocino, CA 95460, tel: (707) 937 5804*). Nearby is working-class **Fort Bragg**, a small city noted for its botanical gardens, the fine fresh seafood 'off the boat' at Noyo Harbor, and the Skunk Train ride to Willits.

For more information, contact the Fort Bragg-Mendocino Coast Chamber of Commerce (*PO Box 1141, 332 N Main St, Fort Bragg, CA 95437, tel: (707) 964 3153*), *open most weekdays 9am–5pm, Sat 11am–4pm*.

South of Mendocino then inland via Highway 128 is the fascinating **Anderson Valley** area, a surviving farming area centred on Boonville. The area is noted for its almost-lost local dialect of Bootling, its Buckhorn Saloon brewpub, and the **Mendocino County Fair and Apple Show** (one of the last non-commercial county fairs remaining in North America).

The Lost Coast

The wild coast north of Mendocino eventually becomes so rugged that the Coast Highway avoids it and veers inland to join Highway 101. For the truly adventurous, California's 'Lost Coast' is accessible via various narrow roads and routes starting from Garberville-Redway, Humboldt Redwoods and Ferndale. For information, stop by state park headquarters at **Humboldt Redwoods** or contact **Sinkyone Wilderness** (*PO Box 245, Whitethorn, CA 95989, tel: (707) 986 7711*).

The redwood parks

The north coast's finest feature, its virgin groves of *Sequoia sempervirens* or coastal redwoods, is best appreciated in Humboldt and Del Norte counties.

Hugging Highway 101 just north of Garberville and Redway is **Humboldt Redwoods State Park**, with 20,234 hectares (50,000 acres) of almost unvisited redwood groves and upland grasslands brushed with mixed conifers and oaks. There are traditional tourist attractions too, especially along the old highway's **Avenue of the Giants**. Most notable, in Meyer Flat, is the **Shrine Drive-Thru-Tree**, one of the state's oldest tourist attractions (wagon trains once drove through it).

Further north, beyond the fascinations of the small Victorian village of **Ferndale** and the attractions of adjacent **Eureka** and **Arcata**, are almost unseen treasures.

Redwood National Park, which now incorporates three exceptional state parks, protects most of what remains of California's original 800,000 hectares (2 million acres) of virgin coastal redwoods (plus much over-logged acreage). Home to three of the world's six largest trees (including the tallest, 112-m (368-ft) 'Howard Libby' Redwood), over 1,000 species of animal and plant life thrive here, including rare Roosevelt elk and (offshore, in season) California grey whales.

Redwood miscellany
For more information, contact:
Humboldt Redwoods State Park
PO Box 100, Weott, CA 95571. Tel: (707) 946 2263 www.humboldtredwoods.org
Redwood National Park
Orick Information Center, PO Box 234, Orick, CA 95555. Tel: (707) 464 6101.

Information about Prairie Creek, Del Norte Coast, and Jedediah Smith redwoods state parks, all included within the national park, is also provided by the Orick Center.

Gracious living at the McCallum House Bed & Breakfast, Mendocino

Walk: Mendocino Headlands

This windswept town on the often fog-shrouded bluffs overlooking the Pacific could easily be mistaken for New England rather than California. In fact, film-makers have been using Mendocino as a New England lookalike since *Johnny Belinda* was made there almost 50 years ago.

Walking is the only way to see Mendocino and this walk explores not only the historic buildings and film trivia but also the wild and rugged coast and beaches of the Mendocino Headlands.

Allow 2 hours

CALIFORNIA NEVAL

• Mendocino
• Napa
• San Francisco

Driving north on Highway 1, turn off at the first Mendocino exit on to Main St. The walk starts at the Presbyterian Church on the left-hand side of the road.

1 Mendocino Presbyterian Church

This is the oldest Presbyterian church in continuous operation in California. In 1947 it was the set for *Johnny Belinda*, starring Jane Wyman.

Continue along Main St, past Lansing St to Kelly House, set back from the street on the right-hand side.

2 Kelly House Museum

Built in 1861, Kelly House is now a Victorian museum and houses the Mendocino Historical Research Library. The town's public toilets are across the road on Main St.

Cross Main St and turn right. Ford House is on the left.

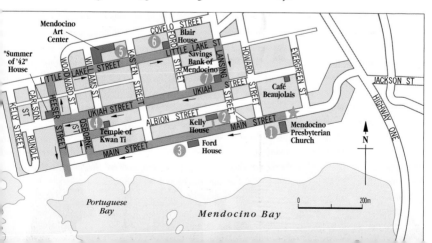

3 Ford House

Also a museum, Ford House was built in 1854 and houses the town's Visitor Information Bureau. There is an excellent large-scale model showing Mendocino as it was early last century. Many of the original wooden buildings of Mendocino have been destroyed by fire, and this is one of the oldest still standing.
Cross Main St again and walk past the boutiques and galleries to Osborne St. Turn right and right again on to Albion St.

4 The Temple of Kwan Ti

This small red building houses an old Chinese temple which can be visited by appointment only (*tel: (707) 937 4506*). *Return to Osborne St, turn right, walk to Ukiah St, turn left and continue to Heeser St. The old house on the right corner of Heeser and Ukiah was the set for the film* The Summer of '42. *Turn right on to Heeser and walk up to Little Lake St. Turn right and continue to Williams St.*

5 Mendocino Art Center

The Art Center has achieved a national reputation and a small gallery has exhibits of both local and national artists.
Continue along Little Lake St to Ford St.

6 Blair House

Mendocino is full of charming bed-and-breakfast inns, and Blair House has the added attraction that it was the location for the television series *Murder, She Wrote*, starring Angela Lansbury.
Continue to Lansing St and turn right. Stay on the right-hand side of the street and walk to the corner of Ukiah St.

7 Savings Bank of Mendocino

This architectural landmark is topped by a superb redwood sculpture of *Father Time*. The building was originally the Masonic Temple.
Turn right on to Ukiah and walk to Heeser St. Turn left, go to Main St and take the trail to the headlands. Steps lead down from the bluff to Portuguese Beach.

Nearby
The **Café Beaujolais**, at the junction of Ukiah and Evergreen streets, is one of the most highly acclaimed restaurants in California. The restaurant is open for dinner only.
Tel: (707) 937 5614.
www.cafebeaujolais.com

Ford House and garden, Mendocino

Getting away from it all

*'I am usually very calm over the displays of
nature, but you will scarce believe how my heart
leaped at this. It was like meeting one's wife.
I had come home again.'*

ROBERT LOUIS STEVENSON
1879

Get a good view from
high up in the sky

Angel Island

This is the largest island in San
Francisco Bay and can easily be seen
to the left of Alcatraz.

Angel Island is covered with forest,
and herds of deer roam free. It was
the Ellis Island of the west, used as a
quarantine station for Asian immigrants.
During World War II it was used as
an internment camp for Japanese
Americans, and the old buildings have
been converted into a museum.

Visit the island for picnics, bicycling
and hiking. The hike around the island
is 10km (6 miles) long and from the
top there are 360-degree views of the
Bay Area. No motor vehicles are allowed
on the island. Access is by ferry from
Pier 41 in San Francisco. It operates
daily in the summer and at weekends
during winter.
Contact: **Blue and Gold Fleet**, *Pier 41,
San Francisco, tel: (415) 705 5555.*

Ballooning

Hot-air ballooning is a popular
diversion in various California locales,
perhaps most notably in Napa Valley.
One company, the oldest wine country
ballooning firm, offers dawn launches
from Domaine Chandon followed by

brunch with sparkling wines. Contact:
Napa Valley Balloons, Inc
*PO Box 2860, Yountville, CA 94599,
Tel: (707) 944 0228* or toll-free in
California *(800) 253 2224.*

For an unusual variation on the
theme, consider 'white-water ballooning'
or the 'splash-and-dash' approach –
a Gold Country experience down,
along, and sometimes in the American
River's south fork. Since pilot Alan
Ehrgott and wife Cindi own a bed-
and-breakfast inn, the bed, breakfast
and balloon package is a bargain.
Contact: **Coloma Country Inn**
*PO Box 502, Coloma, CA 95613,
tel: (530) 622 6919.*

In southern California, the high
desert around Temecula is quite popular
for high-flying balloonists.

Bicycle 'skiing' and tours

In summer, Alpine ski enthusiasts can
schuss down the slopes on mountain
bikes, a popular new pastime now that
many resorts are exploring year-round
recreation options. **Mammoth
Mountain** on the Sierra Nevada's
eastern slope offers 97km (60 miles) of
ski runs 'groomed' in summer for cycle
touring. Guided bike tours, which start

from the Mammoth Mountain Inn, include destinations such as Devil's Postpile and Rainbow Falls as well as Mono Lake and the ghost town of Bodie. Contact: **Mammoth Mountain Bike Park** or **Mammoth Adventure Connection**: *tel: (760) 934 0706 for both.*

Tamer is the Sonoma Valley Tour de Vins, a 24-km (15-mile) trek which offers winery stops and a taste of local history. Contact: **Wheel Escapes** *443 Caenery Street, San Francisco, CA, tel: (415) 586 2377.*

The Blue Goose Murder Mystery

The small steam-powered Blue Goose excursion train in the town of Yreka north of Mount Shasta offers seasonal family fun and a very special summer adventure. An annual summer fund-raising benefit, the day-long Murder on the Blue Goose Express mystery tour, includes train fare, two meals, even a party afterwards. Participants each receive a 'script' for their part in the drama and are expected to wear period attire. Reservations essential. Contact: **Yreka Western Railroad**, *PO Box 660, Yreka, CA 96097, tel: (530) 842 4146.*

Fabulous Filoli

Woodside is a rural oasis on the San Francisco peninsula. This exclusive community close to Stanford is home to one of the great 'stately' homes of California.

The 43-room mansion at Filoli was designed by Willis Polk in 1916 and, although the house is well worth a visit, it is the 6.5 hectares (16 acres) of themed, formal, enclosed gardens that are the main attraction. Eighteen gardeners were required for their maintenance, and none of their former glory has disappeared. Reservations are required for tours: *tel: (650) 364 8300, ext 507.*

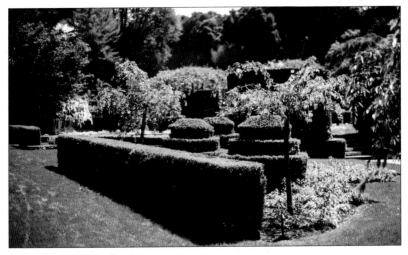

Filoli Gardens, San Mateo County

Farm festivals

Unusual and sometimes highly entertaining in California are the multitude of community farm festivals which have sprouted up and gained tremendous popularity over the years. Most famous, perhaps, is the annual Gilroy Garlic Festival south of San Jose, where 150,000-plus people descend to celebrate the stinking rose with samples of garlic perfume and all-you-can-eat garlic ice cream (a few gallons are usually quite sufficient to feed the entire crowd) as well as big bands and other entertainment.

Other regional festivals include the Artichoke Festival in Castroville, Old Sacramento's Tomato Festival and Garden Bazaar, the Great Monterey Squid Festival, the Brussels Sprouts Festival in Santa Cruz, the Stockton Asparagus Festival, and Watsonville's Strawberry Festival. Even more obscure are events such as Yuba City's Prune Festival, the Colusa Rice and Waterfowl Festival, the Pear Fair in Courtland, and Isleton's Crawdad Festival. California also offers a wide array of colourful ethnic events.

A current events calendar, a listing of ethnic events, and a listing of local chambers of commerce (best sources for obscure events information) can be obtained from **California Tourism** *PO Box 1499, Sacramento, CA 95812, tel: (916) 444 4429. www.visitcalifornia.com*

Kayaking

Perhaps most unobtrusive of all nature touring options is the silently gliding on water. It takes skill, but even novices can learn in a lesson or two to manage most day-long outings (depending on weather conditions). Contact:
Blue Waters Kayaking (trips including Bolinas at Point Reyes, China Camp and Mendocino, *PO Box 983, Inverness, CA 94937 tel: (415) 669 2600. www.bwkayak.com*
Kayak Tahoe *PO Box 11129, Tahoe Paradise, CA 95708, tel: (530) 544 2011;*
Monterey Bay Kayaks *693 Del Monte Ave, Monterey, CA 93940, tel: (831) 373 0119, toll-free in CA, 800 649 5357;*
Sea Trek Trips to Angel Island, Bolinas Lagoon, Drake's Estero, even moonlight dinner runs to Sam's in Tiburon; *85 Liberty Ship Way, Schoonmaker Point, Sausalito, CA 94965, tel: (415) 488 1000.*

Mamas and llamas on the trail

With these unusual beasts of burden carrying most of the load, a llama trip into the Sierra Nevada is an unforgettable experience. One company specialises in environmental education along the trail, hiring university professors and other experts as guides.
Mama's Llamas *PO Box 665, El Dorado, CA 95623, tel: (530) 622 2566.*
Other Sierra Nevada packers and guides, using horses in summer only, operate from eastern slope trailheads. For a listing of reputable farms, contact:
Eastern High Sierra Packers Association *Bishop Chamber of Commerce, 690 N Main St, Bishop, CA 93514, tel: (760) 873 8405.*

Mono Lake and environmental education

The Mono Lake Committee – environmental activists who battle, in the courts and through the media, with Los Angeles Water and Power over the future of the lake's watershed – offers an array of field seminars (from naturalist-led bird and biology tours to weekend study excursions) and classes. Contact: **Mono Lake Committee** *PO Box 29, Lee Vining, CA 93541, tel: (760) 647 6595.* Also contact: **University of California's California Adventures** *2301 Bancroft Ave, Berkeley, CA 94720, tel: (510) 642 4000.* **Yosemite Association** *PO Box 545, Yosemite National Park, CA 95389, tel: (209) 379 2646.*

Riding a skunk in the daylight

The Skunk Train Tour from Fort Bragg to Willits goes back to the area's lumbering heyday. The full 64-km (40-mile) route offers cliff-hanging scenery and sky-high trestle travel through the Noyo River Gulch. The old steam Super Skunk engine chugs out only on Saturday half-day runs; a diesel engine pulls the load on longer and summer outings. On full-day trips, it is also possible to start and end in Willits.

California Western Railroad *PO Box 907, Fort Bragg, CA 95437, tel: (800) 866 1690.*

After appreciating the Willits Station, an architectural work of art crafted from clear-heart redwood, adventurous rail travellers can roll north from Willits to Eureka on the north coast. This is the most spectacular railroad route in California, side-winding through the wild Eel River Canyon slowly enough to watch wildlife, sliding through Scotia and across the Scotia Bluffs, then slipping past the coastal plains farmland to Humboldt Bay. One-way and round trips are available, usually scheduled from late May through to October. **Redwood Coast Railroad Company** *293 E Commercial St, Willits, CA 95490, tel: toll-free 800 482 7100 in California.*

The Skunk Train (California Western Railroad) chugs into the station in Fort Bragg

Ghost towns

The very mention of ghost towns conjures up memories of old Westerns, bleached bones in the desert and tumbleweed blowing through deserted ruins.

California has its fair share of these abandoned settlements. Whenever a mine ran out of gold or silver the town that grew up around it would lose its population. The mines were never in the most hospitable parts of the state and there was absolutely no reason for anyone to live in these God-forsaken places unless there was money to be made.

The buildings usually fell into decay within a few years, and often all that can be found now are rusty tin cans, barbed wire and the overgrown foundations of a few houses, though occasionally some buildings survived. The most popular and accessible ghost town lies just outside Barstow on the road between Los Angeles and Las Vegas.

In 1881 **Calico** boomed with 20 saloons and its own Chinatown. Over $86 million of gold and silver was mined before the mines were exhausted.

Walter Knott of Knott's Berry Farm restored the town and handed it over to San Bernardino County who now operate it as a kind of ghost town theme park. In spite of its blatantly commercial atmosphere, you can still get a feel for the harsh life of the miners in these barren mountains.

In 1904, on the edge of Death Valley, a gold strike near **Rhyolite** resulted in the population growing to 10,000 in a few months. By 1911 the city was reduced to a handful.

Just outside the northwest boundary of Death Valley, Rhyolite today is a group of ruined façades. The front of the Cook Bank Building provides the perfect symbol of a ghost town for photographers, and a few other ruins line the once busy main street. In 1906 Tom Kelly built a house out of 51,000 bottles. Not only is this still standing but it is still inhabited. Inside is an odd collection of antiques and relics.

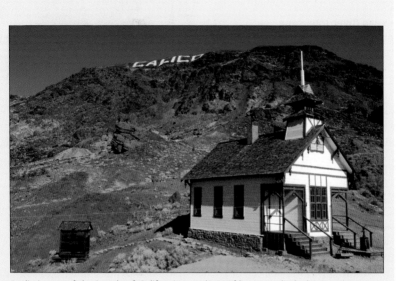

Bodie is one of the jewels of California. High in the Eastern Sierra at the end of a long stretch of dirt road off Highway 395, Bodie stands as a remarkably well-preserved example of a classic ghost town. Until 1876 it was a thriving mining community. Today 170 houses still stand and you can wander through streets that have remained unchanged for decades.

This outdoor museum has been designated a State Historic Park, and, although there has been little renovation, the buildings have been preserved from further deterioration. Many of the buildings are open and many are still complete with furniture and personal belongings. There is a feeling of total authenticity here, particularly when trying to breathe the thin mountain air at 2,590m (8,500ft) as you climb the steep streets. Opposite the town is a cemetery that graphically documents the lives of the miners.

Facing page: the Tom Kelly Bottle House, Calico Ghost Town, Yermo
Above: church at Calico Ghost Town, Yermo; below: abandoned buildings at Bodie Ghost Town, Bodie State Historic Park

Skateboarding on the waterfront walkway near the Casino, Santa Catalina Island

Russian River road tour

Just over an hour's drive north from San Francisco is the Russian River resort area, which first became popular as a retreat for San Francisco's affluent. Those days are long gone, and the Russian River these days is an eclectic cultural collection. Very popular for tours is **Korbel Champagne Cellars** (*tel: (707) 824 7000*) on River Road, a few miles east of Guerneville. Noted for its champagnes, this vintage 1886 red-brick building (lovely gardens) is the only outlet for the company's table wines. Just north of Guerneville are **Armstrong Redwood State Reserve** and adjacent **Austin Creek State Recreation Area** (*tel: (707) 869 2015 for both*).

Some people prefer canoeing: **Burke's Canoe Trips** in Forestville (*tel: (707) 887 1222*) offers quite reasonable day-long tours. Others prefer following the river inland to visit abundant and excellent area wineries. Still others consider the Russian River an annual event and visit only in September, during the very popular **Russian River Jazz Festival** (big-name talent, bigger crowds). Contact: **Russian River Chamber of Commerce** *PO Box 331, Guerneville, CA 95441, tel: (707) 869 9000. www.russianriver.com.* For a free map and brochure about area wineries contact the Russian River Wine Road, PO Box 46, Healdsburg, CA 95448, *toll-free tel: (800) 723 6336.*

Sailing on horseback

The one-time ranch of noted American adventurer and author Jack London is now open to the public, preserved as an exceptional state historic park. With his wife Charmian, London regularly travelled the grasslands and wooded canyons of his beloved Beauty Ranch on horseback. 'I am a sailor on horseback!' he once declared. Especially enjoyable today, and historically appropriate, are the horseback rides offered here. Contact: **Sonoma Cattle Company** *PO Box 877, Glen Ellen, CA 95442, tel: (707) 996 8566.*

In the Russian River's Armstrong Redwoods another company offers half-day to three-day horseback trips, as noted for the campfire cuisine as for the well-mannered mountain-savvy horses. Contact: **Armstrong Woods Pack Station** *PO Box 970, Guerneville, CA 95446, tel: (707) 887 2939.*

In Big Sur, rides in Andrew Molera State Park and longer into the Ventana Wilderness are offered by **Molera Horseback Tours** who have certified guides to navigate this 1,942-hectare (4,800-acre) coastal paradise. Malera Horseback Tours, *Andrew Malera State Park, Big Sur, CA 93920, tel: (831) 625 5486. www.molerahorsebacktours.com*

Spelunking into Midde Earth

California has fascinating caves and caverns to explore, most of them in the Gold Country foothills. All have civilised descent via steps or stairways. A few also allow adventurers to abseil down into the primal darkness.

East of San Andreas, visitors to **California Caverns** (*tel: (209) 736 2708*) can spurn the commercial 'trail of lights' at this state historic landmark and instead squeeze through muddy fissures to reach hidden caves and underground lakes (hardhats, overalls, rafts and guides provided). To the south, near Murphys, **Mercer Caverns** (*tel: (209) 728 2101*) is strictly a family destination. But at **Moaning Cavern** near Angels Camp (*tel: (209) 736 2708*) no experience is required for the more exciting abseil route or full caving tour. (This cave is reputedly the largest in California.) Hundreds of miles north are the **Lake Shasta Caverns** (*tel: (530) 238 2341*). Abseiling or rappelling tours of these colourful caves are by advance booking only.

Santa Catalina Island

A mere 35km (22 miles) off the coast near Long Beach, Santa Catalina Island provides within its 90km (56 miles) of coastline a pristine wilderness that rises to over 610m (2,000ft) in elevation in the interior.

Visitors take the ferry from Long Beach to Avalon, the only town on the island. Maps and information can be obtained from the **Santa Catalina Island Chamber of Commerce** (*tel: (310) 510 1520*). Glass-bottom-boat tours are available from several kiosks along

Avalon Pleasure Pier. The **Santa Catalina Island Company** (*tel: (310) 510 2000*) has night tours when floodlights are used to attract the marine life. The **Catalina Safari Bus** service (*toll-free tel: (310) 510 2800*) drops off hikers at various points around the island. Bicycles can be rented from **Brown's Bikes** at *107 Pebbly Beach Rd, Avalon* (*tel: (310) 510 0986*).

The Wine Train

Intensely disliked in Napa Valley but popular with tourists is the Wine Train. All runs head north from the city of Napa to St Helena, where passengers disembark for winery tours by bus. More expensive trips include food served in the dining cars, while hors d'oeuvres and wine tasting are offered in the lounge cars. Contact: **Napa Valley Wine Train** *1275 McKinstry St, Napa, CA 94559, tel: (707) 253 2111 or toll-free in California (800) 427 4124. www.winetrain.com. Closed: Mon.*

Whale-watching

From mid-December until the end of February, the California grey whale makes its annual 9,656-km (6,000-mile) migration from Alaska to Mexico. They return between March and mid-May.

These huge mammals can be seen from many of the promontories along the coast, or, for a more intimate experience, travel out to meet them in a small boat. Whale-watching cruises are run by several companies, including **The Oceanic Society** (*toll-free tel: (800) 326 7491*) and **New Sea Angler and Jaws** (*tel: (707) 875 3344*).

Shopping

Like most of America, California is a shopper's dream. Not only can you find anything and everything, from popular brand names to unusual imported items, but the price will be attractive too.

Abercrombie & Fitch store at The Grove, Los Angeles

Clothes

Both men's and women's clothes are available in a wide variety of styles and prices from French designer dresses and Savile Row suits to denim jeans. There are some incredible bargains to be found if you know where to look.

JC Penny and **Montgomery Ward** are both department store chains with inexpensive clothes. Nothing here approaches *haute couture* but for work clothes they are difficult to beat.

At the other end of the department store ladder are **Macy's**, **Nordstrom** and **Sak's Fifth Avenue**, which have designer clothes and recognised brand names. These stores often have sales offering good savings. Local newspapers always feature large display ads for these sales.

There are several discount clothing stores that offer the best bargains of all. They all sell name brands, very often designer labels, and often factory seconds. They may not have a wide range of sizes available in all styles but their prices more than make up for the lack of choice.

The cheapest is **Ross Dress for Less** for both men's and women's clothes. For men, **The Men's Warehouse** has very good quality suits and jackets, as do **C & R Clothiers**, and for women **The Clothes Time** has a good selection. Outlet stores are operated by manu-

facturers who feature their seconds and discontinued lines at very low prices.

For the height of fashion and designs from the *couture* houses there is no shortage of shops; Beverly Hills' **Rodeo Drive** is full of them, but do not expect low prices. In San Francisco, **Jessica McClintock** and **Obiko** for women's fashion and **Wilkes Bashford** for men represent this top end of the market.

Electronic goods

Remember that all equipment powered by mains electricity will be for 110v at 60 cycles, but battery-powered gadgets use internationally available battery sizes.

As the home of America's hi-tech industry, California has plenty of computer peripherals and software at bargain prices. Determine compatibility with overseas systems first.

Photographic equipment

The US is currently one of the cheapest places in the world to buy cameras and lenses, but always check on the lowest prices first. The internet is an invaluable source of information. The monthly magazine, *Popular Photography,* carries dozens of ads offering equipment at discount prices. These are usually from New York but they will give an idea of a reasonable price range. Many shops will negotiate rather than lose a sale.

Avoid shops in tourist areas which may try to take advantage of unsuspecting foreigners.

Cameras in the US frequently have a different designation from the rest of the world, but the shop assistant may not know. If you plan to buy an expensive item you should check on the specifications before you leave home.

Remember that the US designation will make it obvious to customs officials where an item was purchased, so keep the receipt handy for when you travel abroad again. It may also void any warranty.

Film of all makes, types and formats is widely available at very low prices.

Books and music

Discounting books has become an accepted practice in the US and many newly published works are available at substantial discounts.

LPs are now virtually unobtainable and cassettes are becoming rarer as CDs gain in popularity. **Tower Records**, **Virgin** and **The Wherehouse** have the best selection and prices.

Souvenirs

Apart from the obvious printed T-shirt and mugs, there is little that is unique to California. **The Disney Store**, not only at Disneyland but also in a dozen other locations throughout the state, has excellent Disney memorabilia. Gold nugget jewellery is a popular souvenir of the Gold Country, and 'grow your own redwood' kits make interesting mementoes – if you have room for the world's tallest tree!

For the sports fan, clothing in the colours of both major baseball and American football clubs is available at most sports outfitters.

Museum shops generally have very high-quality merchandise, well designed, functional and frequently educational.

GREATER LOS ANGELES

Southern California is the home of vast shopping malls. The largest is **Del Amo** in Torrence, and others include the **Glendale Village** and **Santa Monica Mall**. The shops and department stores within these malls are virtually interchangeable.

Beverly Center

This is an eight-acre shopping mall filled with up-market shops, department stores and restaurants.

Farmers' Market

Although farmers are unlikely to make the journey here these days, there are still impressive food displays at over 160 outlets at this open-air complex.

Fisherman's Village

This recreation of a New England fishing village has the usual collection of gift and souvenir shops.

Shopping at Two Rodeo, Rodeo Drive, Beverly Hills

Melrose Avenue

The 6,000 and 7,000 blocks of Melrose Avenue have some of the craziest off-the-wall shops in California. It is all, however, extremely chic.

Olvera Street

In the heart of old Los Angeles is a vibrant, brick-paved street lined with shops and street vendors selling Mexican food and arts and crafts from Mexico.

Ports O'Call Village

This mock 19th-century fishing village has dozens of shops overlooking Los Angeles Harbor at San Pedro.

Rodeo Drive

The name is synonymous with wealth. Window-shopping along this super-exclusive street is enough for most people. Some of the shops even have locked doors and only admit customers by appointment. Nearly every major designer has a shop along Rodeo Drive including Cartier, Gucci and Armani.

Westwood Village

Located next to the UCLA campus, this is the premier shopping area in west Los Angeles. It caters to both college students and fashionable Westside residents. The bookstores are particularly good.

SAN DIEGO

Bazaar del Mundo

This Mexican marketplace within Old Town San Diego State Park has a wide range of colourful Mexican crafts.

Horton Plaza

Not only is this an architectural master-piece, it is one of the best examples of a user-friendly shopping mall in the US. Over 140 shops and restaurants provide for every shopper's need.

Gaslamp Quarter

The old buildings of this historic district are now home to several antique shops and art galleries.

Seaport Village

Over 65 shops occupy this new waterfront development close to downtown San Diego.

SAN FRANCISCO

The Cannery

This converted Del Monte canning factory, close to Fisherman's Wharf, has three floors of boutiques and restaurants centred around a landscaped courtyard.

Crocker Galleria

The Galleria in Milan was the model for this glass-domed collection of 60 fashionable shops selling designer fashions and elegant gifts.

Ghirardelli Square

Ghirardelli still keep a small part of their famous chocolate factory operating, but most of it has been transformed into a multi-level shopping complex with an interesting mixture of boutiques, galleries and restaurants.

Grant Avenue

For eight blocks there are dozens of Chinese craft shops, jewellers and Asian bazaars. Many of the goods are cheap imports, but occasionally you can strike lucky and find a treasure. Remember the

Chinese saying that the best goods are never at the front.

Maiden Lane
Several exclusive boutiques and art galleries line this charming lane off Union Square. The most notable building, No. 140, was designed by Frank Lloyd Wright.

Pier 39
The best street performers in the city entertain the shoppers on this old San Francisco cargo wharf that now has two levels of shops.

San Francisco Center
One of San Francisco's newest shopping experiences is this nine-storey vertical mall crowned by a five-storey branch of Nordstrom's.

Sutter Street
For four blocks, from the 300s to the 700s, Sutter Street has some of the most exclusive fashion boutiques and art galleries in northern California.

Union Street
Not to be confused with Union Square, this street in the Cow Hollow neighbourhood is full of small, fashionable boutiques and curio shops.

Union Square
If San Francisco has a centre, then this is it. All the major department stores are here, including exclusive **Neiman-Marcus**. Just off the square on Post Street, **Gumps** has a range of furnishings, oriental antiques and homeware.

OTHER AREAS
Surprisingly, one of the finest shopping streets in the US, equalling Rodeo Drive in quality, is **El Paseo** in Palm Desert. Art galleries, high-fashion boutiques, jewellers, exclusive antique dealers and fine restaurants all rub shoulders along this extravagant street.

In nearby Palm Springs, the **Desert Fashion Plaza** houses high-class department stores, boutiques and jewellers.

Ghirardelli Square, a place to relax while shopping

Entertainment

In the state that is the centre of the world's film industry, there is no shortage of talent waiting to make its mark on the world of entertainment. It seems that every restaurant in Los Angeles is staffed by actors and actresses just waiting to be discovered.

Classic cars in front of the Sebastiani Theatre, downtown Sonoma

Both London West End and Broadway shows are regularly featured at theatres in Los Angeles and San Francisco, and these are complemented by a multitude of small theatres producing both experimental and traditional drama. Comedy clubs are particularly good.

Music inevitably has a strong representation; many rock stars have made their home in Los Angeles or the San Francisco area. Mill Valley alone, a town of less than 15,000 people, is home to The Grateful Dead, Jefferson Starship, Huey Lewis, Maria Muldur, Sammy Hagar and other great musicians. **The Sweetwater Saloon** on Throckmorton Avenue in Mill Valley features live music every night, and many of these local musicians often drop in to jam with the featured band. Classical fans are well catered for with world-class opera, ballet and symphony orchestras.

Entertainment pages of newspapers usually list and review current events. San Francisco is particularly well served. The Pink Section of the Sunday edition of the *San Francisco Chronicle* has a detailed listing of virtually every event for the week for northern California. Also in San Francisco, the BASS ticket agency has a recorded events calendar (*tel: (800) 225 2277*).

Day-of-performance tickets are available at half price from the **San Francisco Ticket Box Office** in Union Square (*tel: (415) 433 7827*).

In Los Angeles, the *Los Angeles Times* has a daily calendar section that gives complete listings of events and performances in the Greater Los Angeles area.

Throughout the year there are events taking place from county fairs and rodeos to film and jazz festivals. The dates and venues are different every year but the **California Office of Tourism** can provide detailed current listings of all the major events.

Major theatres
LOS ANGELES
Ahmanson Theater
135 North Grand Ave.
Tel: (213) 628 2772.
Coronet Theater
366 North La Cienega Blvd.
Tel: (310) 657 7377.
The Kodak Theater
6801 Hollywood Boulevard.
Tel: (323) 308 6300.

SAN DIEGO
La Jolla Playhouse
UCSD Campus. Tel: (858) 550 1010.

Old Globe Theater
Balboa Park.
Tel: (619) 239 2255.
San Diego Repertory Theater
79 Horton Plaza.
Tel: (619) 544 1000.

SAN FRANCISCO
American Conservatory Theater
405 Geary St.
Tel: (415) 749 2228.
Curran Theater
445 Geary St.
Tel: (415) 551 2000.
Golden Gate Theater
25 Taylor St.
Tel: (415) 551 2000.
Orpheum Theater
1192 Market St.
Tel: (435) 551 2000.

SAN CARLOS
Shoreline Amphitheater
One Amphitheater Parkway.
Tel: (650) 967 3000.

Experimental and fringe theatre
LOS ANGELES
The Actors' Gang Theater
6209 Santa Monica Blvd.
Tel: (323) 465 0566.
Colony Studio Theater Company
555 North 3rd St, Burbank.
Tel: (818) 558 7000.
Actors' Circle Theater
7313 Santa Monica Blvd.
Tel: (323) 882 8043.

SAN FRANCISCO
Theater Artaud
450 Florida St.
Tel: (415) 621 7797.

Comedy clubs
LOS ANGELES
The Comedy Store
8433 West Sunset Blvd.
Tel: (323) 650 6268.
(Also in La Jolla and Westwood.)
The Improv
1862 Melrose Ave.
Tel: (323) 651 2583.

ENCINO
LA Cabaret Comedy Club
17271 Ventura Blvd.
Tel: (818) 501 3737.

SAN FRANCISCO
Cobb's
915 Columbus Avenue.
Tel: (415) 928 4320.
The Punch Line
444 Battery St.
Tel: (415) 379 7573.

Magic
Magic Castle
7001 Franklin Ave,
Hollywood.
Tel: (323) 851 3313.

Classical music, ballet and opera
LOS ANGELES
Pantages Theater
6233 Hollywood Blvd.
Tel: (323) 463 4367.

The Music Center
135 North Grand Ave.
Tel: (323) 850 2000.
Wiltern Theater
3790 Wilshire Blvd.
Tel: (213) 380 5005.

SAN DIEGO
San Diego Opera
1200 3rd Ave.
Tel: (619) 533 7000.
San Diego Symphony
1245 7th Ave.
Tel: (619) 235 0800.

SAN FRANCISCO
San Francisco Opera
301 Van Ness Ave.
Tel: (415) 864 3330.
San Francisco Symphony
Davies Hall, Van Ness Ave.
Tel: (415) 864 6000.

Jazz
The Baked Potato
3787 Cahuenga Blvd,
N Hollywood.
Tel: (818) 980 1615.
2nd Street Jazz
366 East 2nd Street.
Tel: (231) 680 0047.
Pearls Jazz Bar
256 Columbus Avenue.
Tel: (415) 291 8255.
Yoshi's
510 Embarcadero West,
Oakland.
Tel: (510) 238 9200.

Cabaret
LOS ANGELES
Cinegrill
7000 Hollywood Blvd.
Tel: (323) 466 7000.
The Gardenia
7066 Santa Monica Blvd.
Tel: (323) 467 7444).
Largo
432 North Fairfax Ave.
Tel: (323) 852 1073.

SAN FRANCISCO
Great American Music Hall
859 O'Farrell St. Tel: (415) 885 0750.

Dancing and rock
LOS ANGELES
The Viper Room
8852 Sunset Blvd, Hollywood.
Tel: (310) 358 1881.
The Sunset Room
1430 North Cahuenga Blvd.
Tel: (323) 463 8712.
The Palace
1735 North Vine St, Hollywood.
Tel: (323) 462 3000.

SAN DIEGO
Fat City
2137 Pacific Highway.
Tel: (619) 232 9303.
Belly Up
143 S Cedros Ave, Solana Beach.
Tel: (858) 481 9022.

SAN FRANCISCO
Sound Factory
525 Harrison St. Tel: (415) 979 8686.
DNA Lounge
375 11th St.
Tel: (415) 626 1409.

Bimbo's 365 Club
1025 Columbus Ave.
Tel: (415) 474 0365.
Slim's
333 11th St.
Tel: (415) 255 0333.

EVENTS
January
Rosebowl Parade, Pasadena.
February
Chinese New Year, San Francisco and Los Angeles.
March
Santa Barbara International Film Festival.
Santa Cruz Jazz Festival.
April
Redding Dixieland Jazz Festival.
Cherry Blossom Festival, San Francisco.
May
Cinco de Mayo throughout the state.
La Fiesta de San Luis Obispo.
Rodeo week, Redding.
June
Old Globe Shakespearean Festival, San Diego.
Flower Festival, Lompoc.
July
California Rodeo, Salinas.
Carmel Bach Festival.
Steinbeck Festival, Salinas.
Sonoma County Fair.
International Surf Festival – southern California beaches.
August
Mozart Festival, San Luis Obispo.
Monterey County Fair.
September
California State Fair.
Sausalito Arts Festival.
Monterey Jazz Festival.
October
Fleet Week, San Francisco.
Grand National Rodeo, San Francisco.
November
Death Valley Days.
December
Christmas at the Adobes, Monterey.

Children

California is a children's paradise. From Disneyland on there is a multitude of activities to keep even the most jaded children amused for days. It would be impossible to cover everything here as almost every entry in the book would be suitable. Below are listed just a few of the attractions not mentioned elsewhere.

In addition to the major attraction of Disneyland there are also several theme parks that provide endless thrills.

Knott's Berry Farm
The father of all theme parks, next door to Disneyland in Buena Park (see p26). Tel: (714) 220 5200. www.knotts.com. Open: daily, 10am–6pm in winter; 10am–midnight in summer.

Six Flags Marine World
Marine World Parkway, Vallejo. Tel: (707) 643 6722. www.sixflags.com. Call for information.

Paramount's Great America
This park in Santa Clara County south of San Francisco offers an assortment of rides similar to most theme parks, and although the names are different, the quality of thrills remains the same. Great America Parkway, Santa Clara. Tel: (408) 988 1776. www3.paramount parks.com/greatamerica. Open: daily, Memorial Day to Labor Day; weekends during spring and autumn. Closed: winter.

Six Flags Magic Mountain
The ultimate amusement park where, for one-price admission, children (and adults) can get their fill of hair-raising thrill rides. Over 100 rides are spread across 105 hectares (260 acres) and include the Colossus, one of the biggest

and, at 97km/h (60 mph), fastest wooden roller-coasters in the world. Other roller-coasters in the park include Viper, Revolution and Ninja! There are gentler rides for young children, as well as a popular dolphin and sea lion show. 26101 Magic Mountain Parkway, Valencia. Tel: (661) 255 4111. Open: winter, weekends 10am–6pm; summer, daily from 10am.

Winchester Mystery House
Children love the bizarre and spooky atmosphere of the house. It was built by Sarah Winchester, heiress to the Winchester rifle fortune, who believed that she would live as long as the house continued to grow. As a result, by the time she died in 1922 the house had grown to 160 rooms covering 2.5 hectares (6 acres). Doors open on to blank walls, stairways lead nowhere, and ghost stories abound. 325 Winchester Blvd, San Jose. Tel: (408) 247 2101. www.winchestermysteryhouse.com. Open: hours vary with the season.

The Pickle Family Circus performs at different venues in San Francisco throughout the year (tel: (415) 759 8123).

Children's theatre and special events are always regularly held in many parts of the state. Listings of events are carried by most local newspapers.

Sport and leisure

California is the home of champions, a breeding ground for athletes of every kind and state with an unparalleled sports infrastructure churning out some of the world's best athletes. With its nearly ideal weather conditions and its penchant for the pursuit of perfection when it comes to all things physical, California is an athlete's Mecca. It has 14 major professional sports teams, dozens of minor league teams, some of the best collegiate athletics in the country and a huge variety of opportunity for participant sports.

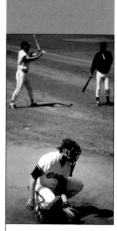
San Francisco Giants on the field, San Francisco

Nearly one-third of American athletes at the 2000 Summer Olympics were native Californians. They won 30 medals – 32 per cent of the US total. Observes author Herbert Gold, 'This Dorado of escapees from elsewhere has produced a new race – the Californian. So much athletic grace is almost unnatural.' To be a good sport in California, you can either do it or just watch it. Whatever you choose, it is all around you.

SPECTATOR SPORTS
American football
No other state can boast having as many professional football teams as California. Four teams from the National Football League take to the field (called the gridiron) every autumn from early September through to late December. Two lucky teams go all the way to the Super Bowl in January.

The **San Francisco 49ers**, with one of the best records in recent football history, play at Monster Park (*tel: (415) 656 4900*). Over the last 20 years Joe Montana remains one of the sport's greatest players ever, having led the 49ers to win four Super Bowl titles.

Because of their great success, getting a ticket to a 49ers game is difficult. They are nearly always sold out.

In Oakland are the **Raiders**, one of the most feared teams in the National Football League because of their aggressive and hard-hitting style of football. They play at McAfee Coliseum, just off the I-880 in Oakland (*tel: (510) 569 2121*).

The **San Diego Chargers** battle on the field at Qualcomm Stadium (*tel: (619) 280 2111*).

College football is also quite enjoyable and accessible. In northern California, both Stanford University (*tel: (650) 497 1021*) and the University of California at Berkeley (*tel: (510) 642 5150*) have strong football traditions. In southern California, the University of Southern California, University of California at Los Angeles and San Diego State University are among a host of college teams to take the field. Southern California also boasts one of football's great traditions, the Rose Bowl, which is held each 1 January between the best teams in the two major athletic divisions. Each year 3,500 seats are sold in a random draw. Send a postcard to: Rose Bowl Ticket Drawing (*PO Box 7122, Pasadena, CA 91109*), postmarked between 15 September and 15 October. For information, *tel: (626) 449 4100.*

Baseball

The American equivalent of cricket takes place at five major baseball league stadiums across California. From April to October, the teams, from both the American League and National League, bat it out on Astroturf and natural grass, playing about 80 home games each.

In the San Francisco Bay area, two of the nation's best teams, the **San Francisco Giants** and the **Oakland Athletics**, play a brand of baseball known as Bays ball. The Giants swing their bats at SBC Park. The Athletics, winners of the 1989 World Series – the famous series that was interrupted by the Loma Prieta earthquake – play in the Oakland Coliseum (*tel: (510) 638 0500*).

In southern California, a strong baseball tradition has grown and transformed at least a portion of the laid-back, beach-going populace into rabid, hot-dog-eating fans of the baseball field.

The **Los Angeles Dodgers** enjoy an outstanding reputation in baseball and often lead the league in attendance. They play at Dodger Stadium.

The **Anaheim Angels** play at the Anaheim Stadium (*tel: (714) 254 3100*) and the **San Diego Padres** play at Qualcomm Stadium (*tel: (619) 881 6500*).

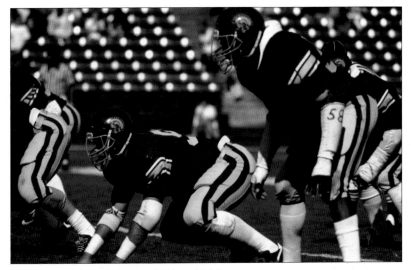

The USC Trojans play at the Los Angeles Memorial Coliseum

Speeding around Infineon Raceway

Basketball

The regular National Basketball Association season runs from October until April, with championship playoffs continuing until May.

The **Golden State Warriors** play at the Oakland Coliseum Arena (*tel: (510) 638 6000*), where they play an average of 40 home games each season. In the state capital, the **Sacramento Kings** are an up-and-coming team, full of enthusiasm, but as of yet they have not been able to muster much in the way of wins.

The **Los Angeles Clippers** are also struggling towards success, but as a young team they have shown promise in recent years.

The reigning champions of California basketball remain the **Los Angeles Lakers**, who play at the Forum in Inglewood (*tel: (213) 673 1300*). One of the greatest teams in the history of American sport, the Lakers have developed a following that literally spans the globe. Jerry West and Kareem Abdul Jabar are among the team's greatest players. But the most famous Laker of all is without question Earvin 'Magic' Johnson, the man who invented such moves as the no-loss pass, the triple double and the coast to coast, but whose career was tragically affected when he was diagnosed HIV positive in 1991.

Ice hockey

In a state where surf and sunshine dominate the landscape, ice hockey, known simply as hockey in the US, seems somewhat out of place. From October to April, the National Hockey League invades California.

The **Los Angeles Kings**, strong championship contenders, play at the Forum in Inglewood. Wayne Gretzky, considered by many to be the greatest player the game has ever seen, joined the Kings in 1989 and has led the team to its greatest record ever. The **San Jose**

Sharks joined the National Hockey League as recently as 1991 and have consistently provided the Bay Area fans with bloodthirsty action with its own brand of Shark Hockey. The Sharks play at the new San Jose arena.

Horse racing

Lady Luck and good old-fashioned love of horses bring thousands of spectators out to California's racetracks, where you can wager as little as $2 on your favourite contender.

In northern California, **Bay Meadows** in San Mateo is one of the state's classic

ovals. Thoroughbred horses race from mid-September to early February, quarter horses run from February to early May. **Golden Gate Fields** holds thoroughbred races from February to late June.

Three tracks dominate activities in southern California. **Hollywood Park** hosts thoroughbred races from April to July and harness racing from August to December.

Santa Ana Park holds thoroughbred races from December to April, while the season at the **Del Mar Track** in San Diego runs from mid-July to early September.

Motor racing

Every April, the US Grand Prix for 500cc motorcycles takes place at **Laguna Seca** near Monterey. Long Beach holds a grand prix for Indy cars every year, and in San Diego, at the Del Mar racetrack, there are IMSA car races which are the equivalent to European Class C cars.

Infineon Raceway near Napa holds race meets for both cars and motor-cycles from February to September. The popular NASCAR championship takes place here, as does the SCCA TransAm Race. A racing school operates through-out the year for budding racing drivers.

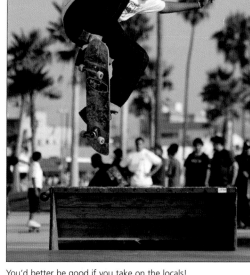

You'd better be good if you take on the locals!

PARTICIPATORY SPORTS
Golf

If you decide to bring your clubs on holiday, you will not be disappointed. Golf is a year-round sport in nearly all parts of California, and almost every city and town has a public golf course. In southern California alone there are more than 200 public courses; of course several of these stand out and deserve special mention.

Pebble Beach near Carmel is a world-class resort with world-class views and world-class prices. Green fees are $300 per player! Everything else at this semi-private resort, owned by Japanese interests but on state-owned land, is also expensive. Yet the scenery and the challenging course are magnificent and definitely a once-in-a-lifetime experience for the avid golfer.

A tremendous assortment of other public courses dots the California landscape and includes: **Silverado Country Club** in Napa, **Tilden Park** in Berkeley, **Cypress Point** in Monterey, **Sean Ranch** near Mendocino, **Rancho Park Golf Course** (the site of the Los Angeles Open), **Torrey Pines Municipal Golf Course** in La Jolla and the **Palm Springs Municipal Golf Course**.

The *Yellow Pages* has listings of both public and private golf courses.

Tennis

California is tennis crazy. At nearly every school and every park in California, players both old and young practise their skills in what might be the nation's leading tennis state. From Pancho Gonzales and Jack Kramer to Tracy Austin and Billie Jean King, California has dominated the sport of tennis, at both professional and amateur levels.

The *Yellow Pages* lists private clubs and occasionally public courts. Many towns have municipal courts and these can be found by telephoning the appropriate parks and recreation departments listed under the Government Pages in the telephone directory.

More information on tennis can be obtained from the **Northern California Tennis Association** (*tel: (510) 748 7373*) or the **Southern California Tennis Association** (*tel: (310) 208 3838*).

Skiing

Whether you are a downhill skier or a cross-country skier, California has some of the finest conditions in the US. From November to May, skiing in the Sierra Nevada has gathered a national following. It is almost always better than the cold, icy and crowded ski slopes of the East Coast; it is often every bit as good as the famed Rocky Mountain skiing.

The Lake Tahoe region, with 20 ski areas and 160 lifts, boasts the highest concentration of skiing in the US. Resorts include **Squaw Valley**, **Heavenly Valley**, **Kirkwood** and **Alpine Meadows**.

Further south is **Mammoth Mountain**, on the eastern side of the Sierras. It is one of the continent's largest ski areas, with 30 lifts and more than 150 trails, and with a vertical drop of 1,006m (3,300ft). Nearer Los Angeles, an assortment of ski areas includes **Mount Baldy**, **Big Bear**, **Snow Summit**, **Mount Waterman** and **Krata Ridge**.

Cross-country skiing is also very popular in the Sierras. You can ski at a touring centre such as the **Kirkwood Touring Center** near Lake Tahoe. For the more intrepid, a trip into the back country in one of the state's many mountain parks and reserves is a possibility.

OTHER SPORTS

Watersports are very popular during the summer, including **kayaking** and **white-water rafting**. **Surfing**, together with **windsurfing**, still enjoy tremendous popularity, and **scuba-diving** trips are available at many places along the coast. In the wine country **ballooning** is a popular pastime, and several companies offer champagne flights in the early morning. **Hang-gliding** courses are available along the coast for the more adventurous.

Cycling has gained in popularity since the development of the mountain bike. Many national forests and state parks have designated bike trails.

Horses can be rented at stables located throughout the state, particularly in the coastal areas where the horses can be ridden along the beach.

Fishing, last but certainly not least, is the state's most popular pastime, and almost every stretch of water, both fresh and sea, will have an angling club close by. Rods and other equipment are usually available for hire by the day at very reasonable rates.

Wherever there is a harbour along the coast someone will be offering fishing charters. Listings of operators can be found in the *Yellow Pages* under 'Fishing Parties'. Salmon is the most popular catch, followed by rock cod and bass.

Freshwater fishermen have the choice of steelhead, salmon, sturgeon and trout. Most of the mountain areas have fitters offering fishing trips, and these can again be found in the *Yellow Pages*.

For current information on fishing licences and seasons, contact the **Department of Fish and Game** (*1416 Ninth Street, Sacramento, CA 95814, tel: (916) 445 0411*).

See also Getting away *on pp140–43.*

Conquering the greens in Escondido

Food and drink

Without any exaggeration, there is virtually no cuisine on earth that cannot be found in California. San Francisco alone has over 4,000 restaurants, even more per capita than New York. Californians enjoy eating, not just for the sake of it but for the love of it. It is a state of 'foodies' who have helped California become one of the world's great gastronomic centres.

Inside a Chinese restaurant, San Francisco

Fine restaurants abound, and not just in the cities. Oakhurst lies between Fresno and the High Sierra, in the middle of nowhere, but even here there is a restaurant that the eminent American gastronome Craig Clairborne deems worthy of visiting – from New York!
Erna's Elderberry House ★★★★
(*tel: (559) 683 6800*) is the unlikely name for this outstanding European restaurant which serves a nightly fixed menu with a choice of either vegetarian or non-vegetarian fare.

It is ridiculous, however, to suggest that all California restaurants are good. There are vast numbers of eating establishments that rely more on quantity than quality and serve unimaginative, greasy American food at its worst.

Some American eating habits are curious, to say the least. Biscuits are like scones and they are usually served smothered in thick white gravy – very often for breakfast! The use of fruit is interesting too. Fruit is considered an appropriate accompaniment to any meal, so do not be too surprised when your bacon and eggs are served with a fruit salad on the same plate.

Some restaurant language can be confusing, so here is a short course on menu translation:
Au jus usually applied to beef sandwiches served with a dip of beef juices
BLT toasted bacon, lettuce and tomato sandwich
Broiled grilled
Brownie individual chocolate cake
Buffalo wings chicken wings in a hot and spicy sauce
Chips potato crisps
Cider a non-alcoholic apple drink
Club sandwich a double-decker sandwich
Eggs benedict popular brunch dish of poached eggs on a slice of ham and an English muffin, covered in Hollandaise sauce
English muffin a muffin
Entrée main course
Fries chips
Half-and-half half milk, half cream
Hash browns fried grated potato
Home or steak fries thick chips often made with unpeeled potatoes, sometimes cooked with onion and spices
Jello jelly
Jelly jam
Mayo mayonnaise

Muffin an individual cake, often made with bran and blueberries

Pancakes thick batter pancakes, served for breakfast with butter and syrup

Prime rib standing rib of beef served in thick slices

Pudding a soft, whipped dessert, often of chocolate

Sherbet sorbet with a milk base

Soda any soft drink

Sub submarine – long sandwich made with French bread or a soft roll

Sweet and low non-sugar sweetener for coffee, etc.

The best breads are made by the Boudin bakery

Elegant interior at Erna's Elderberry House

Fast food

Fast-food chains abound and many of them are so international that they have become synonymous with American food. **McDonald's, Kentucky Fried Chicken** and **Pizza Hut** (all ★) dominate the world market and they are equally dominant in California. They will provide very cheap, fast food in hygienic surroundings. Fortunately, American tastes and attitudes have been changing in the past decade and the greasy hamburgers with French fries (chips are potato crisps) are now having to compete with chicken breast sandwiches and salads. Even the traditional beef fat for frying French fries has been replaced with vegetable oil in most places.

There are several McDonald's look-alikes, including **Wendy's**, **Burger King** and **Jack in the Box** (all ★). They all provide variations of the same products at more or less the same price.

Coffee shops

The coffee shop chains are one step above the fast-food operations and include **Denny's**, **Bobs Big Boy** and **Baker's Square** (all ★★). While they all serve perfectly edible food, it will never be memorable. They are often open 24 hours a day and are absolutely predictable. To experience one Denny's is to know them all. They all have inexpensive children's menus and you need never feel embarrassed at having screaming children at your table.

One of the better chains, not really in the coffee shop category except in price, is **Fresh Choice** (★). One of the best eating bargains in California is their all-you-can-eat fruit and salad bar where,

for a ridiculously low price, you can fill yourself on fresh fruit and every kind of fresh salad imaginable. They also cater for children. **The Sizzler** offers a more restricted salad bar but adds steaks, chicken and seafood to the menu.

Diners

The diner is a very American institution and even lent its name to a film. Although they are less common in California than the East Coast there are a few about in most towns. They are not a lot different from coffee shops. They are generally smaller, with a long counter to sit at. The traditional diner was designed to look like a railroad dining car with lots of chrome and always a juke box. They always served good, basic, cheap food wthout any frills. There are still a few of these around, but beware; California, trendy as ever, has taken the diner to new heights. **The Fog City Diner** ★★★ (*tel: (415) 982 2000*) in San Francisco, for example, is a yuppiefied version of the original, serving dishes such as grilled pasilla pepper with avocado salsa, and crabcakes with a sherry-cayenne mayonnaise. Great food, but hardly your average diner!

Breakfast

Diners and coffee shops (not the chains) are the best places for breakfast, and it is often served 24 hours a day. Eggs are the mainstay and, apart from omelettes, scrambled, boiled and poached eggs, they can be fried either:

Sunny-side up – cooked on one side only.

Over easy – flipped over so that the

white is fully cooked but the yolk is still runny.

Over medium – one step beyond the above.

Over hard – both the white and yolk are solid.

The eggs are invariably served with hash-brown potatoes, a choice of sausage, ham or bacon, and a choice of white or wheat bread or an English muffin.

At weekends breakfast is eclipsed by brunch at the better restaurants. Usually served between 10am and 3pm, this leisurely meal is just a glorified breakfast accompanied by champagne.

Coffee is the main breakfast-time brew and it varies dramatically in quality from brown water to something a spoon will stand up in. The cheaper the restaurant the weaker the coffee is a good rule of thumb. This may have something to do with the American tradition of serving unlimited coffee for a single price. The pot is bottomless and your cup will be refilled for as long as you sit. Tea is less popular and it is easy to see why. A cup of tea consists of a tea bag in tepid water. Water will continue to be provided until no more colour can be drained from the bag.

Every part of the meal involves decisions. There is nothing as simple as a cup of tea. Do you want Darjeeling, English Breakfast, Earl Grey, Camomile, Constant Comment, Ginseng? The list goes on and on and on. You want milk in it. How about half-and-half, 1 per cent, non-fat, regular vitamin D, non-dairy creamer?

One reason for all this choice is the abundance of produce available in California. As the bread-basket of the nation there is more variety of fresh fruit and vegetables here than in any other state.

In the southern part of the state is a huge citrus industry. The Central Valley grows everything from avocados to kiwi fruit. Every year there are festivals attracting thousands of people to sample such unlikely dishes as garlic ice cream at the **Gilroy Garlic Festival**. Monterey has a Squid Festival, Castroville hosts an **Artichoke Festival** and Ventura has a slightly more appealing annual **Strawberry Festival**.

Fresh produce is always close at hand and the Pacific provides fish of all shapes and colours. Dungeness crab comes into San Francisco Bay along with swordfish, shark, red snapper, tuna, salmon, squid and many others.

Rockin Robins on Haight Street

BEVERAGES
Wine

The other major crop in California is grapes. The wine industry extends from the great vineyards of Napa and Sonoma up to Lake and Mendocino Counties in the north and as far south as San Diego. Excellent wines are made near Santa Cruz and Santa Barbara that are the equal of many European fine wines. Many of the grapevines in fact descend from European stock. For example, in Napa Valley the original grapevine cuttings were supplied by priests from the missions at Sonoma and San Rafael.

Most of the California wines are made from a single variety of grape, unlike European wines which are often blends. The wine is named according to the variety, and two that the Californian wine-makers excel at are Cabernet Sauvignon and Chardonnay, but there are several other varieties that are eminently drinkable.

No wine lover should leave California without tasting a good Zinfandel, a grape variety unique to North America. Some of the best Zinfandels are made by Ravenswood and Ridge wineries. A popular trend has been for wineries to follow fashion and produce a white Zinfandel. This rosé wine is pretty to look at but bears little relationship to the big, spicy and fruity red Zinfandels, even though the grape is the same.

Wines are available in any supermarket, any drugstore and, of course, specialised wine merchants. The enormous displays can be confusing to the uninitiated. In restaurants ask for advice, and do not be embarrassed to send the wine back if you think the advice was bad. In shops, on the display, there is often a description and rating of the wine by either a magazine called *The Wine Spectator* or Robert Parker, a well-known American wine writer. The ratings are somewhat controversial because of their subjectivity, but they provide a pretty reliable guide to quality. Generally, any wine that scores over 90 will be good.

Sampling grapes in the vineyards, Sonoma County Wine Country

In cheaper restaurants, particularly outside the main urban areas, the choice will be red, white or burgundy. All will be served straight from the refrigerator. The red could be white Zinfandel or an equally insipid rosé. It is unlikely that any of them will be drinkable.

Beer

America's contribution to the wine industry unfortunately did not spill over to beer. To Europeans, American beer is fizzy and tasteless. Fortunately, in California there are alternatives. Almost every restaurant and bar will have imported beers available. Heineken and Carlsberg are the most common, but the Mexican beers are more interesting and include Dos Equis, Corona, Bohemia and Tecate.

Northern California produces several of the best beers in the US from small local breweries. Sierra Nevada Ale from Chico and San Francisco's Anchor Steam Beer are both excellent. There has been a recent trend in microbreweries with beer made on the premises. If you can find one of these it is worth a try.

Other drinks

In non-alcoholic drinks colas lead the market. Both Coca-Cola and Pepsi are universally available along with 7-Up, Sprite and Dr Pepper, and they are all available in a sugar-free version. Root beer has a loyal following and connoisseurs rank A&W as one of the best. For the more sophisticated palate, California has several different mineral waters that are either plain or flavoured with different fresh-fruit juices. The most common are Calistoga and Crystal Geyser.

This potent Mexican spirit is made of the distilled fermented juice of an agave plant

Bars

Most restaurants serve wine and beer, but only a few of the more expensive ones have a full liquor licence, allowing them to sell hard spirits. The American bar is certainly a place for serious drinking. They are almost always dark and have a decidedly decadent air to them. They always seem the kind of place you would not want your mother to see you enter.

Bars generally open as early as 6am and stay open until 2am. Many bars will advertise a 'Happy Hour' between 5pm and 7pm when drinks are often two for the price of one, and in the better bars free *hors d'oeuvres* are served. The food is sometimes so good that it can be a good substitute for dinner.

Where to eat

The restaurant business has always been precarious and has become increasingly so in the present economic climate. New restaurants open and close with monotonous regularity. Apart from the inexpensive chains, all of the restaurants mentioned here are well established but tend to be more expensive than most. Always ask locally for recommendations of current popular restaurants.

The following table is an indication of restaurant price. The ★ sign indicates the approximate cost per person of a three-course meal without wine.

★	under $15
★★	under $25
★★★	under $50
★★★★	over $50

Compared with Europe, even the most expensive restaurants will seem reasonably priced.

California cuisine

The revolution in cooking in California started with a small group of northern California chefs who developed dishes using the freshest possible local ingredients and presented them with a simple elegance. Many Americans used to plates groaning with food criticise the small portions often associated with this American *nouvelle cuisine*.

Chez Panisse ★★★★
Alice Waters' restaurant in Berkeley is still a gastronomic Mecca. It serves a fixed menu nightly and reservations must be made weeks in advance.

To experience the cooking without the expense, go upstairs to the **Cafe at Chez Panisse ★★★**, an à la carte restaurant that does not take reservations. The wait can be long but the food is worth it.
1517 Shattuck Ave, Berkeley.
Tel: (415) 548 5525.
L'Amour dans le Four ★★
Authentic French food baked or grilled and spiked with a lot of love and personal attention. Offers a very reasonable 'early bird special' and live music two nights a week. Located in the Marina with parking facilities nearby.
1602 Lombard St, San Francisco.
Tel: (415) 775 2134.

The plush interior of a San Francisco restaurant

Fine dining awaits you in California

PosTrio ★★★★

Wolfgang Puck's San Francisco outpost, this elegant restaurant serves consistently good food.
545 Post St, San Francisco.
Tel: (415) 776 7825.

Spago ★★★★

Puck's most famous restaurant is in West Hollywood. Along with Chez Panisse, this represents the pinnacle of California cuisine.
1114 Horn Ave, Los Angeles.
Tel: (213) 652 4025.

East-west cuisine

A recent trend has been to combine elements of both fine Oriental and Western cooking. A few restaurants have done this with great success, such as:
Chinois on Main ★★★★
2709 Main St, Santa Monica.
Tel: (213) 392 9025.

Restaurants of the world

The ubiquitous Chinese restaurant excels in California, particularly in San Francisco where a huge Chinese community supports some of the best in the world. Drop into almost any of the tiny restaurants scattered throughout Chinatown and the Avenues for delicious Chinese food from virtually every kind of produce.

Japanese restaurants abound in both the LA and San Francisco Japantowns. They are completely authentic and serve everything from noodle dishes to fresh sushi. **The Benihana of Tokyo** chain (★★★) cook food at the table, and what the food lacks in imagination is more than compensated for by the entertainment. Italian restaurants are extremely popular throughout California and range from very inexpensive to ultra deluxe, but a broad middle range serves good food.

French restaurants have gained in popularity in recent years and they are generally in the higher price bracket. The best are as good as you can find anywhere.

For value, the Southeast Asian restaurants cannot be beaten. Vietnamese and Thai food is almost always very reasonably priced and very good. It is usually very spicy, but if you ask they will tone it down. Wherever you decide to eat in California you will almost certainly eat well and for much less than you would pay for the equivalent meal at home.

Luscious desserts with fresh, local fruit

Hotels and accommodation

California has an enormous choice of accommodation, from budget to super-luxury, and it is all comparatively inexpensive compared with much of the rest of the world. It is also of an almost universally high standard. Even the cheapest places are clean and well appointed. This does not include inner-city residential hotels which cater for transients and often look as though they went out of business decades ago.

The Hyatt Regent, San Francisco

Motels

The motel, of course, is the American lodging *par excellence*. For the budget-conscious traveller, these are by far the best places to stay. They can be unbelievably cheap and they are never very expensive (often just $50–100 per night.

The chain motels are perhaps the most predictable for quality but they fill up quickly so it pays to book ahead. They all provide a clean, simply decorated room, usually with the choice of twin or double beds. There is always a television, a telephone in all but the most basic, and always a bathroom or shower and toilet en suite.

The difference between the cheapest and the next category up is very slight. There may be a swimming pool and you may get a sachet of shampoo in the bathroom but these refinements can cost $20–$30 more without any basic increase in comfort. Payment is usually in advance and rooms will be held only until 5pm unless the reservation is secured with a credit card.

Motels tend to be on the outskirts of town on the main roads, and are rarely in the best locations for sightseeing. If you have a car this is not a problem. Motels are usually well advertised with huge roadside signs. Most towns have a motel strip; in San Francisco it is Lombard Street, and any local should be able to tell you where to go.

Breakfast is never included but there is usually a restaurant close by and vending machines for soft drinks. Complimentary coffee is sometimes provided in the reception lobby. Good, very inexpensive chains are:
Motel 6 *Tel: 800 466 8356.*
Days Inn *Tel: 800 325 2525.*
Super 8 *Tel: 800 800 8000.*
Also very good but not as cheap are:
Travelodge *Tel: 800 255 3050.*
Comfort Inn *Tel: 800 228 5150.*
Vagabond Inn *Tel: 800 522 1555.*
Best Western *Tel: 800 528 1234.*
Howard Johnson's *Tel: 800 654 2000.*
(All these numbers are toll-free.)

Full-service hotels are much more expensive than motels and they are generally only found in the major cities.

Staying in style

California also has some of the great classic hotels of the world for those who can afford them ($200–500 per night):

In San Diego: the Hotel del Coronado and the Valencia.

In Los Angeles: the Biltmore, Beverly Wilshire, Bel Air and Beverly Hills Hotel.

In San Francisco: the Fairmont, the Mark Hopkins, Westin St Francis and the Palace Hotel.

In Santa Barbara: the Biltmore.

In Yosemite: the Ahwahnee.

Even in hotels of this quality breakfast is rarely included in the price, although there is a growing trend to include a continental breakfast at some hotels.

Also at the top end of the market are resort hotels that not only provide deluxe service and surroundings but also a range of sports, including tennis and golf, and often spa facilities. Once you have checked into one of these luxury resorts there is no reason to set foot in the outside world again until your money runs out.

Some of the best in this category include:

La Costa near San Diego.

Ritz-Carlton at Laguna Niguel.

La Quinta near Rancho Mirage.

Lodge at Pebble Beach.

Meadowood Resort in Napa Valley.

Sonoma Mission Inn and Spa.

Claremont Resort in Berkeley.

Regent Beverly Wilshire Hotel, Beverly Hills

Holiday Inn, downtown San Francisco

Most of the big international hotel chains have properties in California and these provide a more reasonably priced alternative ($100–200 per night) without the glamour of a landmark building. They are usually well located near main tourist attractions.

Hilton *Tel: 800 445 8667.*
Hyatt *Tel: 800 233 1234.*
Sheraton *Tel: 800 325 3535.*
Ramada *Tel: 800 228 2828.*
Holiday Inn *Tel: 800 465 4329.*
Marriot *Tel: 800 228 9290.*
Doubletree *Tel: 800 528 0444.*
(All these numbers are toll-free.)

Bed and breakfast

Northern California has a growing number of bed and breakfast inns. You can find them in Carmel, San Francisco, Napa Valley, the Gold Country and Mendocino. Do not be deceived. These are not the budget seaside accommodations of Europe with rates of $100–250 per night. In California they can be more expensive than some hotels. They are all superbly appointed and usually very romantic. The Victorian motif of most places is a big selling point with Californians who are hungry for history, however recent.

For a list of inns in California send an SAE to **Bed and Breakfast International** (*151 Ardmore Rd, Kensington, CA 94707*). From outside the US, enclose an International Reply Coupon.

Getting the best value

When making reservations for any accommodation make sure it is in a convenient location. Ask plenty of questions. It is also worth asking if there are any special rates available. Many places will give significant discounts rather than lose the business; it never does any harm to ask.

Several chains offer discounts if vouchers are purchased outside the US. These include:

Howard Johnson's Freedom North America, Vagabond Discover America Hotel Pass and **Tourcheck America**, who handle bookings for Best Western, Hilton, Holiday Inn, Ramada, Travelodge and Quality Inn.

Most travel agents should be aware of these programmes and have vouchers available for purchase.

Long-distance calls from in-room telephones can be marked up by quite outrageous amounts and there is often a charge for just using the phone for reverse charge (collect) or credit card calls. Always find out what these charges are to avoid a nasty shock when it is too late. All hotels and motels have public telephones available in the lobby areas. Many hotels do not charge for local calls, but, paradoxically, it is usually the cheaper places that have this policy. Again, check before use.

In-room mini-bars are another big profit centre for hotels. Drinks are so cheap in California that if you enjoy a nightcap it is almost as cheap to buy a full bottle at a supermarket as it is to buy a miniature from a mini-bar.

Hostels

Very low-cost accommodation ($20–30 per night) is available in both YMCA/YWCA hostels (known as 'Y') or in Youth Hostels (AYH). The 'Ys' are only found in larger cities, but the 'AYHs' are located in most tourist centres and hiking areas.

A complete listing can be found in the *International Youth Hostel Handbook*, or contact **American Youth Hostel Association** (*PO Box 37613, Washington DC 20013*). For information on YMCAs look in the telephone directory.

The Achilles Heel, Haight Street, San Francisco

Practical guide

Arriving
Documents

All travellers must be in possession of a valid passport. British citizens arriving by air are granted a visa waiver, but will need a visa if arriving in the US by other means. To travel visa free your passport must be machine readable (for further detail visit *www.usembassy.org.uk*). Citizens of Australia and South Africa also require visas, which should be obtained in your country of residence. Visas are free and last the life of your passport. American immigration laws are strict, and if you have any queries consult your nearest US Consulate before departure. Whilst in the US visitors can take a side trip overland or by sea to Canada or Mexico and re-enter the US without a visa within the 90-day period. This rule also applies to nationals of Andorra, Belgium, Netherlands, Luxembourg, Denmark, Finland, France, Germany, Iceland, Italy, Japan, Liechtenstein, Monaco, Norway, San Marino, Spain, Sweden and Switzerland. Immigration laws are strictly enforced. Check with the American Embassy well before departure.

By air

Los Angeles International is the main airport for international flights into southern California, handling over 60 airlines; San Diego is smaller and it is used by some international charter companies. San Francisco International serves northern California, with Oakland and San Jose handling some charter flights.

Domestic flights are generally very expensive, with the exception of the services between San Francisco and Los Angeles. If planning short hops within the state or flying in from another state, it is advisable to purchase a ticket before arrival. Several airlines offer Visit USA passes, and travel agents should be able to advise on the best deals.

Virtually all California's commercial airports have all the facilities a traveller would expect, although only the major airports will have banking facilities. Disabled travellers are usually well provided for. Services available for business travellers include conference rooms and a wide range of communications facilities.

At both Los Angeles International and San Francisco International there is a wide range of choice for transport into town. There are several taxis, buses and car rental companies. Airporters offer a door-to-door service for much less than a taxi but take longer as they carry other passengers and make frequent stops. Most major hotels in the vicinity of the airports offer a free shuttle service.

Airport taxes are included in the price of the ticket.

Major airline telephone numbers

Air Canada *Tel: 800 776 3000.*
Air New Zealand *Tel: 800 262 1234.*
American Airlines *Tel: 800 433 7300.*
British Airways *Tel: 800 247 9297.*
Continental Airlines *Tel: 800 525 0280.*
Delta Airlines *Tel: 800 221 1212.*
Frontier *Tel: 800 432 1359.*
Jetblue *Tel: 800 538 2583.*
Northwest Airlines *Tel: 800 225 2525.*

Qantas *Tel: 800 227 4500.*
Southwest *Tel: 800 435 9792.*
USAir *Tel: 800 428 4322.*
United Express *Tel: 800 241 6522.*
(All these numbers are toll-free.)

Camping

The Californian climate lends itself to camping holidays and outside the major cities there is no shortage of campsites.

National and state parks have excellent camping facilities but reservations must be made during the peak season. This is the summer for most of the state and winter for the deserts. Some parks impose 7- to 15-day limits during these periods. Reservations at state parks can be made through:

Reservations, Department of Parks and Recreation *Box 942896, Sacramento, California 94296–0001, tel: (916) 653 6995.*

For national parks campsites contact:
National Park Service *Fort Mason, Building 201, San Francisco CA 94123, tel: (415) 556 0560.*

Some of the best campsites are in California's 18 National Forests. Reservations can be made up to 120 days in advance by telephoning *800 283 2267 (toll-free).* For information on the camp sites contact: **USDA Forest Service** *630 Sansome Street, San Francisco CA 94111, tel: (518) 885 3639.*

Back-country camping is allowed in the national parks, but wilderness permits must first be obtained from the park. Bears can be a serious problem and there are strict rules concerning storage of food. Never ignore the warnings and rules laid down by the park service.

There are many private campsites that generally have more sophisticated facilities than those in the parks. They cater particularly for camper vans and motor homes, providing both water and electricity hook-ups. A directory on private campgrounds is available from: California Travel Parks Association (*PO BOX 5648, Auburn, CA 95604, tel: (530) 885 1624*).

On-site tent hire is not generally available, but equipment can be bought inexpensively from sports shops.

Camper vans are available for hire in major towns. In the US they are called motor homes and they are not available from regular car hire sources. One of the biggest companies is **Cruise America** (*tel: 800 671 8042 toll-free*). Local firms are listed under 'Motor Home – Renting and Leasing' in the *Yellow Pages.*

Children

Throughout the state children are well catered for. Many hotels provide cots (cribs) at no extra charge, and extra

Airport shuttle services are cheap

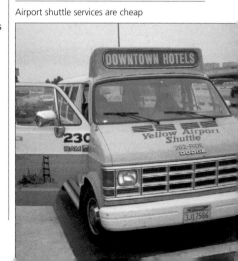

beds for older children are available at a nominal charge. Larger hotels offer babysitting services that are safe and reliable. Many restaurants have children's menus or offer children's portions from the main menu. High chairs are universally available.

Food and nappies (diapers) for infants are available in profusion at any supermarket or drugstore, and in most towns they will be available 24 hours a day from at least one convenience store. Baby milk is called infant formula and is available in several dairy and non-dairy varieties. Prices are very reasonable.

California is generally safe for tourists, but never leave children unattended.

Climate
The best months for travel are generally April to June and September to November. In July and August the temperatures can be sizzling in the deserts of southern California and cold and foggy on the north coast and in San Francisco. December to March is usually wet and cold. During these months, however, the snowfall in the high Sierra provides world-class skiing, and when it stops snowing the skies are usually blue.

The winter is the best time to visit the deserts, and in March the flowers will be starting to bloom.

Weather Conversion Chart
25.4mm = 1 inch
°F = 1.8 x °C + 32

Consulate Generals

Australia *575 Market Street,*
Suite 1800, 18th Floor,
San Francisco, CA 94105.
Tel: (415) 536 1970.
Canada *550 S Hope Street,*
Los Angeles, CA 90071.
Tel: (213) 346 2700.
Ireland *100 Pine Street, 3rd Floor,*
San Francisco, CA 94111.
Tel: (415) 392 4214.
New Zealand *2425 Olympic Boulevard,*
Suite 600E, Santa Monica, CA 90404.
Tel: (310) 566 6555.
United Kingdom *11766 Wilshire*
Boulevard, Suite 1200,
Los Angeles, CA 90025.
Tel: (310) 481 0031.
1 Sansome Street, Suite 850,
San Francisco, CA 94104.
Tel: (415) 981 3030.

Crime

Crime is a very real problem but should be put into perspective. It is at its worst in the big cites but not really any worse than in many other major cities throughout the world.

General availability of handguns is one of the major problems, but the chances of even seeing a gun, other than on a policeman's hip, are very remote. Most shootings are in areas that tourists would rarely visit. However, it is unwise to get into a confrontational situation with anyone, particularly while driving. Frayed tempers have often been known to result in shootings. It is also unwise to pick up hitchhikers.

A more real problem is theft, from both cars and hotel rooms. Take sensible precautions and make sure valuables are not blatantly on display. Most hotel thefts are opportunist, and the more difficult it is to snatch something and run the less chance it will be stolen.

It is wise to carry traveller's cheques rather than cash. All hotels and most shops and restaurants will accept US dollar cheques which can be purchased before leaving home. Thomas Cook, VISA and American Express traveller's cheques are widely recognised and provide fast service in the case of loss or theft.

Shopping is usually trouble-free. Prices for consumer goods in the US are generally much better than in other parts of the world, but care should be taken in some tourist areas, particularly with cameras and electronic goods. Buy an appropriate magazine and look at the small ads in the back. You may not be able to equal the prices you find there, which are often for New York stores, but it will give you a good idea of the general range.

Good protection can be obtained if you pay for items by credit card. If the goods are unsatisfactory the charge can often be disputed later with the credit card company.

Customs regulations

Everyone entering the US must pass through US customs. Personal allowances for visitors include one quart (0.9461 litres) of spirits or wine, 300 cigarettes or 50 cigars, plus up to $100 worth of gifts. In practice, most of these items are far cheaper within the US than at airport duty-free shops so there is little point importing them.

There is no restriction on the amount of currency imported or exported, but anything over $10,000 must be declared.

US customs are particularly concerned about drugs, animals, meat (both fresh and processed), plants and fresh fruit. Penalties are severe.

Driving
Accidents

1. Set up warning signs. Flares are usually used in California and are available from any auto store.
2. Call police and an ambulance if required. The emergency telephone number is 911.
3. Take the names and addresses of all involved, make and licence plates of the other vehicle, and the names and numbers of insurance policies.
4. Write down names and addresses of any witnesses, together with the time and date of the accident. If possible, take photographs of the accident from several angles.
5. Under no circumstance admit to or sign any statement of responsibility.

Breakdown

The American Automobile Association (AAA) is a member of a worldwide association of motoring organisations (AIT) and as such makes certain services available to visitors of member organisations. Both roadside assistance and free route maps are available upon presentation of your membership card. The Triple A operates a nationwide road service number (*tel: 1-800-AAA-HELP*) which will give you information on obtaining emergency assistance. Should you break down on a highway, lift up the bonnet (hood) of your car and remain in the vehicle until the Highway Patrol arrives. Do not open your doors or windows to anyone else.

Car hire

Every airport, however small, will have at least one car rental company associated with it. The major airports have several. All the major companies are represented (Hertz, Avis, Budget, National and Dollar) but there are hundreds of local companies that often offer better rates. Generally, off-airport companies offer the best value and they all provide a free shuttle service to their facility. There are dozens of listings in the *Yellow Pages*.

It is usually better to arrange for a car before arriving. Several airlines have special deals available with preferential rates if the booking is made in advance. It is always better to make a reservation if possible, as certain categories of car may be in short supply during peak seasons.

Automatic transmission is standard on all rental cars. American cars are big and a so-called mid-size is huge by European standards. The smallest size available is the sub-compact which will carry just four people and a small amount of luggage. For summer travel, ask for a car with air-conditioning. It should be available at no extra cost.

None of the major car rental companies will rent to anyone under the age of 25. It may be possible to find a local company that will, but be prepared to pay a loaded insurance premium.

Extra collision insurance will always be offered and this can be almost 50 per cent of the rental fee. You may already be covered by your own personal car insurance policy. Check before leaving home.

In cases of breakdown immediately inform the car rental company and await instructions.

Documentation

Drivers will need a valid licence from any country signatory to the 1949 Geneva Agreement. International Driver's Permits are generally unnecessary.

Major roads are well surfaced and well signed.

Driving tips

Americans drive on the right-hand side of the road. Because of the low speed limits, freeway driving is generally safe. In cities there is a continual problem with drivers anticipating traffic lights or trying to make it through on amber. Always be careful at these junctions.

There are many minor junctions where there is a stop sign in only one direction and they are often not clearly marked. Pay particular attention when driving off the main roads. Road signs use international symbols.

In Los Angeles it may be wise to plan your journey ahead of time. The freeways can be so complicated that a missed turn-off can result in a lot of frustration and lost time. (*See also pp16–17 for more details.*)

Petrol

California is a car-oriented state and there is no shortage of petrol stations and garage facilities. Petrol, called gas, is available in 87, 89 and 91 octane. Diesel is also available at most gas stations.

All gas stations have good maps for sale and most car rental companies will have local maps available free of charge.

Speed limits

Inter-city motorways are called freeways and other roads are highways. The speed limit on all highways and freeways is 89km/h (55mph) unless otherwise posted. It is 105 or 113km/h (65 or 70mph) on rural freeways. In town the limit is between 40 and 56km/h (25 and 35mph). Speed limits are strictly enforced. On freeways you can theoretically be ticketed for driving too slowly in the left hand lane, but this rarely happens.

For more details on Driving *and* Parking *see pp16–17.*

Al fresco in Frisco

Electricity

The standard supply is 110 volts at 60 cycles. Adapters are readily available for purchase in the US but it may be easier to bring one from home to save time finding a shop that sells them.

Emergency telephone numbers

Police, **Fire** and **Ambulance** *911*.

Health

There are no specific health requirements for visitors to California. The standard of health care is extremely high but so are the costs, and it is essential to have a good insurance policy. Many doctors and hospitals will refuse to give treatment unless proof of insurance can be given. All major hospitals have 24-hour emergency rooms.

Information on doctors can be obtained from hotels or listings in the *Yellow Pages*.

California does not have many specific health problems. Tap water is drinkable but, if hiking, do not drink water from the streams, as it often carries the parasite Giardia.

AIDS is a continuing concern, particularly in the San Francisco area. The AIDS Hotline telephone number here is *(415) 863 2437*. Needless to say, safe sex is an absolute necessity.

Hitchhiking

Hitchhiking is only illegal on freeways. However, it is not recommended in California. Motorists are very wary of hitchhikers.

Insurance

Travel insurance to cover both loss of property and medical expenses is highly recommended. Make sure that medical policies give adequate cover, including emergency flights home. Cancellation insurance is advisable if appropriate.

'Cable car' tour of downtown San Francisco

Laundry

All major hotels have one-day laundry and dry-cleaning services from Monday to Friday. Alternatively, there are many dry-cleaning shops offering a two- to four-hour service. Check *Yellow Pages*.

Maps

General maps are available from car hire companies. More detailed town maps and walking maps are usually available free of charge at Chambers of Commerce or Visitor Bureaux, which will be listed in the telephone *Yellow Pages*. Detailed trekking maps are on sale in the National Park Visitor Centres.

Measurement and sizes

California still uses the imperial system of measurement.

Media

The closest there is to a national daily newspaper in California is the *Los Angeles Times*. In northern California the *San Francisco Chronicle* is the major daily, but it tends to be rather parochial. In most towns you can find both the *Wall Street Journal* and the *New York Times*, which often give a more global view of the news.

For local news, including weather and

Conversion Table

FROM	TO	MULTIPLY BY
Inches	Centimetres	2.54
Centimetres	Inches	0.3937
Feet	Metres	0.3048
Metres	Feet	3.2808
Yards	Metres	0.9144
Metres	Yards	1.0940
Miles	Kilometres	1.6090
Kilometres	Miles	0.6214
Acres	Hectares	0.4047
Hectares	Acres	2.4710
Gallons (uk)	Litres	4.5460
Litres	Gallons (uk)	0.2200
Gallons (us)	Litres	3.7854
Litres	Gallons (us)	0.2642
Ounces	Grams	28.35
Grams	Ounces	0.0353
Pounds	Grams	453.6
Grams	Pounds	0.0022
Pounds	Kilograms	0.4536
Kilograms	Pounds	2.205
Tons	Tonnes	1.0160
Tonnes	Tons	0.9842

To convert back, for example from centimetres to inches, divide by the number in the third column.

Men's Suits

UK		36	38	40	42	44	46	48
Rest of Europe	46	48	50	52	54	56	58
USA		36	38	40	42	44	46	48

Dress Sizes

UK		8	10	12	14	16	18
France		36	38	40	42	44	46
Italy		38	40	42	44	46	48
Rest of Europe	34	36	38	40	42	44
USA		6	8	10	12	14	16

Men's Shirts

UK	14	14.5	15	15.5	16	16.5	17
Rest of Europe	36	37	38	39/40	41	42	43
USA	14	14.5	15	15.5	16	16.5	17

Men's Shoes

UK		7	7.5	8.5		9.5	10.5	11
Rest of Europe	41	42	43	44	45	46
USA		8	8.5	9.5	10.5	11.5	12

Women's Shoes

UK		4.5	5	5.5	6	6.5	7
Rest of Europe	38	38	39	39	40	41
USA		6	6.5	7	7.5	8	8.5

traffic conditions, keep the car radio tuned to one of the news stations. There is a radio station for virtually every interest from classical to rap, and there is also what is known as 'talk radio', which attracts calls from the fringes of society and is usually banal at best. It can, however, provide an amusing diversion and an insight into the American psyche.

In most parts of the state it is possible to receive a Public Broadcasting Service (PBS) station. The quality of programming is considerably more intelligent than the other networks and they carry the BBC News.

Virtually every hotel and motel room in the state will have a television. More often than not, it will be cable TV offering 30 or more channels. The problem is finding one worth watching. As with radio, there are usually two or three PBS stations that give good news coverage, even if most of the other programmes are second-hand from British TV.

The newspapers all carry full TV guides, but there are no radio listings and you just have to keep trying until you find a station you like.

Money matters

Banking hours have traditionally been from 10am–3pm Monday to Friday, but recent competition has resulted in longer opening hours and even Saturday opening. There is no longer a general rule, except that the 10–3 core period is the same.

Most banks do not offer foreign exchange facilities, but it is possible to exchange money at the airport or hotel.

It is useful to have small-denomination cheques when using them as cash.

The US dollar bill is available in denominations of 1, 5, 10, 20, 50 and 100. There is a two-dollar bill but it is rarely seen. Be very careful, as all notes are exactly the same size and same colour. It is better to avoid the higher denomination to avoid expensive mistakes. Coins come in denominations of 1 cent (penny), 5 (nickel), 10 (dime) and 25 (quarter). Always keep a few quarters (25 cents) handy for parking meters, telephones and newspapers.

All major credit cards are universally accepted.

Sales tax is applied to all goods and restaurant meals within California. An additional 7–8.5 per cent (depending upon the county) will be added to the price tag.

There are no restrictions on the amount of money that can be either brought into or taken out of the US (*see* Customs Regulations *p177*).

National and state holidays

1 January New Year's Day
January, 3rd Mon Martin Luther King Day
February, 3rd Mon President's Day
May, last Mon Memorial Day
4 July Independence Day
September, 1st Mon Labor Day
October, 2nd Mon Columbus Day
11 November Veteran's Day
November, 4th Thur Thanksgiving
25 December Christmas Day

Government offices, including post offices, are closed for most of these holidays, but few people observe them all. Shops remain open on all but Thanksgiving and Christmas. Peak periods for travel, hotels and campsites are Memorial Day, Independence Day and Labor Day. Air travel peaks at Thanksgiving and Christmas.

Opening hours

Most larger shops are open seven days a week, typically from 10am to 6pm and from noon on Sundays. Smaller shops and more specialised businesses close on Sundays.

Most offices, including government offices, open Monday to Friday, 9am–5pm.

Museums and art gallery timings vary dramatically. Recent budget deficits have resulted in severely curtailed opening hours at many state museums, and it is always wise to check before a visit.

Organised tours

The majority of people visiting California hire cars, which is undoubtedly the best way to see the state. If time is limited a tour may be the best solution. Particularly in cities, tours can remove the headache of searching for parking spaces, and will also ensure that all the major sites are covered.

There are both regular and specialised tours available in the three major cities. If time is limited, a regular tour may fit the bill, but it will be with a large bus-load of tourists on a fairly superficial trip. The specialised tours cater for specific interests and are usually with smaller groups of people.

Dozens of tour operators serve California, and hotels will usually be able to give advice on what is available.

Two Wells Fargo Bank ATMs along the sidewalk

Regular tours of Los Angeles are given by **LA Sightseeing Tours**. **Tower Tours** operate in San Francisco, and in San Diego **San Diego Scenic Tours** offer 4-hour tours of the city.
Los Angeles *Tel: (310) 458 0257*
San Francisco *Tel: (888) 657 4520*
San Diego *Tel: (858) 273 8687.*

Specialised tours

Cable Car Charter's motorised 'cable cars' pick up passengers every half hour from Pier 41 in San Francisco for either a Heart of San Francisco or Golden Gate Bridge tour. The tour is very basic but the transportation is interesting, even if not authentic (*tel: 800 562 7383, toll-free*).

Pharmacies

Most pharmacies are open from at least 9am until 6pm, and many have longer hours. Drugstores will have a pharmacy counter for dispensing prescriptions, and these are usually open until 9pm. Drugstores are like mini-supermarkets and have a wide range of products on sale including wine and spirits, hardware and snacks.

Yellow Pages gives a complete list of pharmacies.

Many non-prescription drugs can be obtained from regular supermarkets.

Places of worship

It seems that every religion known to mankind has a place of worship in California.

The state is predominantly Catholic and every neighbourhood has a Catholic church.

Newspapers generally list times of services for the main denominations, and a complete list can be found under 'Churches' in *Yellow Pages*. In the San Francisco area alone there are ten pages of churches. This blanket listing covers mosques and Buddhist temples but not synagogues, which have their own listing.

Police

Every incorporated city in California has its own police force with normal police responsibilities including traffic control. An incorporated city can have a pop-ulation as small as 500, though the average is 2,300.

The areas outside the cities are policed by the county sheriff, a different title but essentially the same job except that they have no jurisdiction over traffic. That is the function of the California Highway Patrol. In the case of any emergency throughout the state the telephone number to call is *911*.

Post offices

Post offices are generally open Monday to Friday from 9am to 5pm. They are always closed on Sundays.

Stamps are available from vending machines in some hotels and shops, but they will cost more than from a post office. Postage rates change frequently, so always check on current tariffs.

An airmail letter or postcard takes about one week to travel from California to Europe. Surface mail can take three months! Parcels must be properly packaged and, if being sent by registered mail, non-removable, non-shiny tape must be used. Appropriate containers are sold at the post office. A customs declaration form must accompany any parcel being mailed abroad.

Poste Restante is known as 'General Delivery'. Letters can be addressed to any post office and must include the zip code.

Mail will only be held for 30 days, after which it will be returned to the sender, whose name and address must be on the envelope.

When collecting general delivery mail you will need some form of identification.

Post boxes are called mail boxes and are blue with 'US Mail' in white lettering.

Telegrams are sent from Western Union Offices, not from post offices. If you have a credit card you can dictate a telegram over the telephone and charge it. Western Union Offices are listed in *Yellow Pages*.

Public transport

The majority of Californians drive cars, and outside San Francisco the public transportation system, with the exception of air travel, is not well developed.

By air

All the main towns in California have commercial airports. Between San

Francisco (SFO) and Los Angeles (LAX) there are flights virtually every half-hour on several different airlines. Other destinations have much less frequent services. The SFO–LAX route is like a bus service, with reasonably priced tickets. Other routes are much more expensive, and it is usually better to buy tickets before arriving in the US.

The whole airline business is in such a state of flux that only a travel agent will be able to give current, comprehensive information on flights and fares.

By bus

Bus travel is cheap but the distances are so great that, unless your budget is really tight, it wastes valuable time. An additional problem is that the long-distance bus stations tend to be in the less desirable parts of town. Some of the passengers on these buses can also leave a lot to be desired. You would not want to share a football stadium with some of the characters who use these buses, never mind a seat!

Greyhound is a major operator travelling between all the main cities. On some routes such as Los Angeles–San Francisco, Greyhound is not significantly cheaper than the cheapest air ticket. For the greatest saving buy an Ameripass which is available for 4–60 days' duration. Buy tickets online at *www.discoverypass.com* at least 21 days in advance of travelling. Local Greyhound offices in California can be found in *Yellow Pages.*

An alternative to Greyhound is Green Tortoise which runs weekly trips between Los Angeles and San Francisco at a very reasonable price. It caters

Green-and-yellow National taxi cab

particularly for students and younger people. In Los Angeles and San Francisco the telephone number is *(415) 956 7500.*

By train

The rail system in California is not well developed. However, all major cities are connected, and Amtrak trains are clean and comfortable if not particularly fast.

Discount rail passes are available at Amtrak stations in Los Angeles and San Francisco on the production of your passport. Reservations must be made on all trains in addition to holding the pass.

Other transport

Taxis are available in all towns of any size but are quite expensive.

In San Francisco, cable-car rides are a must, but these days they are as much a tourist attraction as a means of transport. Only three lines are now in operation (*see p83*).

In the San Francisco Bay area The Bay Area Rapid Transit (BART) provides a fast, efficient underground train service between San Francisco and the East Bay. It links eight city stations with 25 in the East Bay.

The ferries are the most pleasant way to travel across the bay. The Red and White fleet (*tel: (415) 673 2900*) operates between San Francisco, Angel Island, Tiburon and Vallejo. The Golden Gate Ferry Service (*tel: (415) 455 2000*) runs between San Francisco and Sausalito.

In San Diego the 'Tijuana trolley' makes the 26-km (16-mile) journey to the Mexican border every 15 minutes throughout the day and links several San Diego communities.

Thomas Cook timetables

Details and times of long-distance bus and train services can be found in the *Thomas Cook Overseas Timetable,* available to buy online at *www.thomascookpublishing.com,* from Thomas Cook offices in the UK, or by calling *01733 416477.*

Senior citizens

Most hotels, motels, restaurants and museums have preferential rates for senior citizens. Usually they want to see some form of identification, but often just looking old enough will work (which can, however, be very demoralising!).

Smoking

California, always a leader in social trends, has almost banned smoking. It is not allowed on public transport or in any public buildings. Smoking is not permitted in offices, or in bars and restaurants.

Many hotels offer non-smoking rooms and car hire companies offer smoke-free cars.

Smokers are generally looked upon as social pariahs and they are rapidly becoming the exception rather than the rule in California.

Sustainable tourism

Thomas Cook is a strong advocate of ethical and fairly traded tourism and believes that the travel experience should be as good for the places visited as it is for the people who visit them. That's why we firmly support The Travel Foundation, a charity that develops solutions to help improve and protect holiday destinations, their environment, traditions and culture. To find out what you can do to make a positive difference to the places you travel to and the people who live there, please visit *www.thetravelfoundation.org.uk*

Telephones

In California telephones are everywhere and most of them work. Apart from telephone kiosks there are public telephones in most bars, restaurants and hotel lobbies. You are never far from a phone.

All public telephones accept 5, 10 and 25 cent coins, with 25 cents being the minimum change. In airports there are often telephones that allow the call to be charged to a credit card.

Hotels usually charge a high premium for calls from rooms. Conversely, some hotels allow local calls at no cost. Always check the rates to avoid an unpleasant surprise when checking out.

Reverse charge calls, called collect calls, can be made from any telephone by calling the operator. Dial *0* for the local operator or *00* for long-distance.

All numbers with an *800* or *877* prefix are toll-free. At a public telephone insert a dime first (10c) which will be returned when you hang up.

For international calls dial *001*, the country code and then the number (without the first 0 of the area code). The cheapest time for transatlantic calls is between 11pm and 7am.

International codes
Australia *61*
Canada *no country code from US*
Ireland *353*
New Zealand *64*
United Kingdom *44*

Local directory information *411*
Long-distance directory enquiries (area code) *555 1212.*

MUNI bus at bus stop in San Francisco

Telephone booths on the street

Time

California is on Pacific Standard Time, which is eight hours behind GMT. From the last Sunday in April to the first Sunday in October daylight saving time is in operation, when the clocks are put forward by one hour.

Tipping

Tips are a way of life and everyone in the service industry expects them. They are very rarely included in the bill except occasionally in restaurants when there is a large party. Always check.

The amount is, of course, always at the discretion of the customer, but this is a general guide:

Restaurants and bars 15 per cent
Cloakroom attendants $1
Parking valet $1
Airport porters (skycaps) $1 per bag
Taxi drivers 15 per cent
Tour guide or driver $1 per day
Hotel porter $1 per bag
Room maid $2 per day
Hotel parking valet $1
Room service 15 per cent
Hairdresser 10 per cent
Shoe shine 50 cents
Toilet attendant 50 cents

Toilets

Public toilets, called rest rooms, are not always easy to find, but when you do they are almost always clean and free. In cities they can be found in large department stores, bars and restaurants, and all petrol stations.

Tourist offices

For general information on California contact:

California Office of Tourism *801 K St, STE 1600, Sacramento, CA 95812* (*tel: (916) 322 2881*). They can provide maps, comprehensive brochures and referrals to local Chambers of Commerce for more specific information.

San Diego San Diego International Visitor Information Center, *11 Horton Plaza, CA 92101* (*tel: (619) 236 1212*).

Written requests for information should be sent to:
San Diego Convention and Visitors Bureau, *1200 Third Avenue, Suite 824, Dept 700, CA 92101.*

Orange County Anaheim Visitor and Convention Bureau, *800 West Katella Avenue, Anaheim, CA 92892 (tel: (800) 598 3200. www.anaheimoc.org)*

Greater Los Angeles Area Greater Los Angeles Visitor and Information Center, *685 Figueroa Street, CA 90017 (tel: (213) 689 8822. www.lacvb.com)*

Palm Springs Area Palm Springs Visitor Information Center, *2901 North Palm Canyon Drive, CA 92262 (tel: 800 347 7746 toll-free. www.pschamber.org)*
Palm Springs Desert Resorts Conventions and Visitors Bureau, *Atrium Design Center, 70–100 Highway 111, Rancho Mirage, CA 92270 (tel: (760) 770 9000. www.palmspringsusa.com)*

Central Coast Santa Barbara Conference and Visitors Bureau, *1601 Anacapa Street, Santa Barbara, CA 93101 (tel: (805) 966 9222. www.santabarbara.com)*

San Francisco Bay Area San Francisco Information Center, *Hallidie Plaza, Lower Level, Powell and Market streets, San Francisco, CA 94101 (tel: (415) 391 2000).*
Written requests for information should be sent to:
San Francisco Convention and Visitors Bureau, *201 Third Street, Suite 900, San Francisco, CA 94103. www.sfvisitor.org*

High Sierra Lake Tahoe Visitors Authority, *1156 Ski Run Boulevard, PO Box 16299, South Lake Tahoe, CA 95706 (tel: 800 288 2463 toll-free. www.virtualtahoe.com)*

North Coast Redwood Empire Association, *2 Beach Street, San Francisco, CA 94133. Tel: (415) 292 5527. www.redwoodempire.com*

Travellers with disabilities

California is more responsive to the needs of disabled people than many places.

At airports there are always good facilities including special lifts, toilets and availability of wheelchairs.

Most hotels, public buildings and museums now have wheelchair access and toilet facilities. Any public building erected or renovated since 1982 is required by law to have extensive facilities for the disabled, including access and toilets. It is always a good idea to check with your destination to verify that adequate facilities are available.

Handicapped parking areas are widely available and hefty fines are given for illegal use of these spaces. They are always marked in blue and with a wheelchair symbol.

Throughout the state people will be sympathetic to the problems of disabled travellers and generally very helpful.

What to take

Most people find that they take too much to California. You can find everything you can get at home and more, and it is generally cheaper. Clothes are particularly good value. The best advice is to leave plenty of room in your suitcase for the many bargains that you will inevitably want to take home with you.

ACKNOWLEDGEMENTS
Thomas Cook Publishing wishes to thank the following libraries and associations for their assistance in the preparation of this book, and to whom the copyright in the photographs belongs.

MARY EVANS PICTURE LIBRARY 30a; FRED GEBHART AND MAXINE CASS 1, 2, 4, 5, 6, 10, 11a, 11b, 12, 13, 14a, 14b, 15a, 15b, 16, 17, 21, 22, 23a, 23b, 24, 25, 26, 27, 28, 30b, 31a, 31b, 33, 36a, 36b, 37a, 37b, 38, 40, 41, 43a, 43b, 44a, 44b, 50, 51, 52, 53, 55, 56, 57, 58, 59a, 59b, 61a, 61b, 62, 64, 65, 67, 68, 69, 71, 73, 74, 75, 77, 80a, 80b, 81a, 81b, 82, 83, 86, 87, 92a, 92b, 93b, 97, 98, 99, 100, 101, 102, 103, 105a, 105b, 106a, 108, 109, 111, 113, 114a, 114b, 115a, 115b, 116, 118, 120, 122, 123, 124, 125, 126, 127, 128a, 128b, 129, 130, 131, 133, 134, 135, 137, 139, 140, 141, 143, 144, 145a, 145b, 146, 148, 149, 152, 156, 161, 162, 163a, 163b, 166, 171, 183, 188; ROBERT HOLMES 11b, 23a, 23b, 26, 37a, 87, 157, 158, 163b, 169a, 169b; PICTURES COLOUR LIBRARY 93a, 159

The remaining pictures are held in the AA PHOTO LIBRARY and were taken by: BARRIE SMITH with the exception of pages 106, 107 and 187 which were taken by HAROLD HARRIS and page 167 which was taken by PETER WILSON.

Index: MARIE LORIMER

Proofreading: JAN McCANN for CAMBRIDGE PUBLISHING MANAGEMENT LIMITED

Send your thoughts to
books@thomascook.com

We're committed to providing the very best up-to-date information in our travel guides and constantly strive to make them as useful as they can be. You can help us to improve future editions by letting us have your feedback. If you've made a wonderful discovery on your travels that we don't already feature, if you'd like to inform us about recent changes to anything that we do include, or if you simply want to let us know your thoughts about this guidebook and how we can make it even better – we'd love to hear from you.

Send us ideas, discoveries and recommendations today and then look out for your valuable input in the next edition of this title. And, as an extra 'thank you' from Thomas Cook Publishing, you'll be automatically entered into our exciting monthly prize draw.

Emails to the above address, or letters to Travellers Project Editor, Thomas Cook Publishing, PO Box 227, Unit 18, Coningsby Road, Peterborough PE3 8SB, UK.

Please don't forget to let us know which title your feedback refers to!